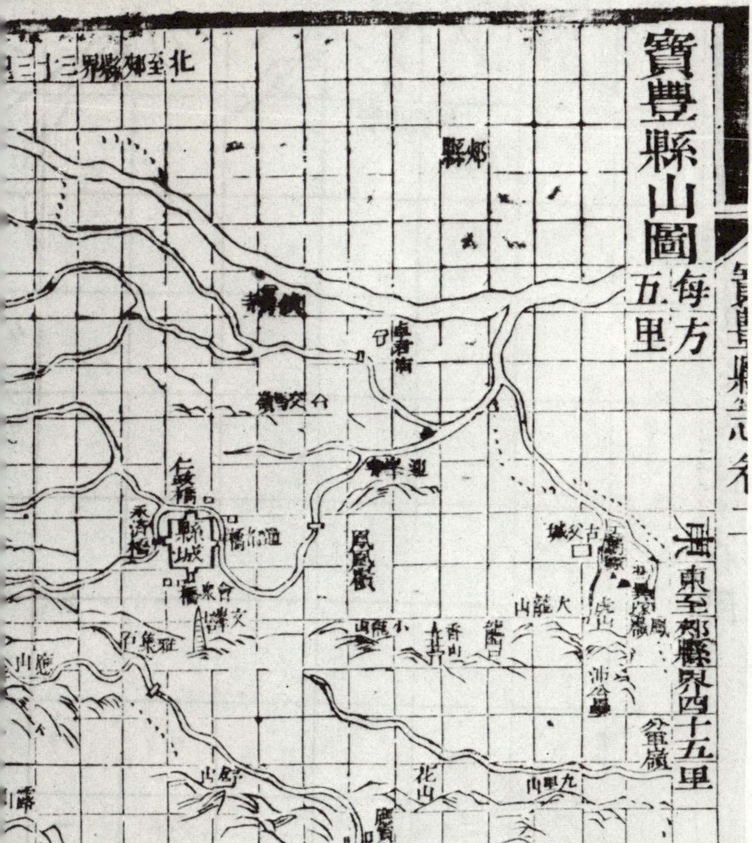

The Legend of Miao-shan

Glen Dudbridge

Published by
Ithaca Press London
for the Board of the Faculty
of Oriental Studies
Oxford University
1978

OXFORD ORIENTAL MONOGRAPHS No 1
Copyright © Glen Dudbridge 1978
First published in 1978 by
Ithaca Press 13 Southwark Street London SE1
for the Board of the Faculty of Oriental Studies
Oxford University

ISBN 0 903729 38 5

Printed in England by Anchor Press Ltd
and bound by Wm Brendon & Sons Ltd
both of Tiptree Essex

Contents

1. Introduction — 7
2. The Kuan-yin cult at Hsiang-shan ssu — 10
   2.1. The monastery and Chiang Chih-ch'i — 10
   2.2. The birth of the legend — 15
3. Versions of the story to 1500 — 20
   3.1. The idea of a written tradition — 20
   3.2. The version by Tsu-hsiu — 22
   3.3. Thirteenth-century references — 36
   3.4. The version by Kuan Tao-sheng — 39
   3.5. The early growth of a *pao-chüan* tradition — 44
4. The sixteenth and seventeenth centuries — 51
   4.1. The *Nan-hai Kuan-yin ch'üan-chuan* — 51
   4.2. Saints' lives in the late Ming — 58
   4.3. First signs of a theatrical tradition — 61
   4.4. The Spanish evidence — 65
   4.5. Reinterpretations — 68
5. Anatomy of the story — 74
   5.1. Annotations — 75
   5.2. 'King Lear' — 79
   5.3. Development before and after 1100 — 81
6. Interpretations — 85
   6.1. A charter for celibacy — 85
   6.2. A supreme act of filial piety — 89
   6.3. Miao-shan in the world of the dead — 92
   6.4. Concluding remarks — 97
Notes — 99
Appendix — 117
List of works cited — 118
   Abbreviations — 118
   Primary sources — 118
   Secondary sources — 121
Index — 125

Acknowledgements

I am indebted to many colleagues and friends for the stimulus of their comments on the ideas proposed in this book. In particular I am glad to acknowledge the many ways in which my Oxford colleague Piet van der Loon has helped my research on this subject over the years: with suggested material, with hours of discussion on questions both technical and general, and with a critical reading of the finished work. I would also like to thank Wang Ch'iu-kuei, of the National Taiwan University, who generously provided me with copies of source material and bibliographical information, and two British anthropologists, Marjorie Topley and Barbara Ward, who in letters and discussions have helped me to clarify certain ideas. Any imperfections which remain are of course my own responsibility.

Above all I thank my wife Sylvia for the moral support and the many forms of practical assistance she has given to make the publication of this book possible.

G. Dudbridge

1 Introduction

IN 1575 the Spanish Augustinian friar Martín de Rada (1533–1578) spent two months in Fukien as head of a mission which we now regard as one of the significant early contacts between Europe and China. At one point in his report on the visit, commenting on those whom the Chinese 'revere as saints', he noted that 'the one whom they honour most is a woman called Quanyin, daughter of a king called Tonçou, who led a solitary life and a holy one after her fashion'.[1] He had heard a legend of Kuan-yin which we find set out at greater length by one of the military officers in his party, Miguel de Loarca:

> Quanim ... was daughter of the king Tzitzonbon, who had three daughters, and married off two of them. He wanted to have Quanim married too, but she would never consent, saying that she was bound to live in chastity. Upon this her father grew angry and put her in a monastery. There she was made to carry water and firewood, and to clear up a kitchen garden that was in the monastery. But the Chinese relate that the monkeys came from the mountain and helped her, the saints of the monastery carried the water, the birds cleared up the garden with their beaks, and the great beasts came to carry the wood for her. Her parents, seeing this and imagining that it was witchcraft, as indeed it must have been, gave orders to set fire to the monastery. And she, seeing that because of her they were burning it and the statues of the saints that were there, would have cut her throat with a silver pin which she was wearing to tie up her hair, but then there

came about a great storm of rain which put out the fire, and she went and hid herself in a mountain where they say she did great penance. And the King her father, for the sin which he committed against her, was consumed by leprosy and worms. Seeing himself thus, he made a proclamation throughout all his kingdom. And, no physician having been able to heal him, the daughter, who learned of it, came from the mountain where she had been to heal him, without his recognising her. And as all his limbs were putrid she removed one of her own limbs and herself put it on him in the diseased place. And when she had healed him in this way she was left lacking her main limbs, and the father, now well, at last came to recognise her and felt grief to see her thus without her limbs. But she consoled him and became whole again as before. Then the father, seeing this miracle, bowed down to the ground and began to worship her. She would not allow it, but seeing that her father persisted in his worship she took an image of a saint and put it on her head, so that they would understand that her father was worshipping the saint's image and not herself. And immediately she returned to the wilderness, where she died leading a solitary life. They esteem her as a great saint and petition her to get them pardon for their sins from Heaven, for that is where she is.[2]

When, a few years later, Juan González de Mendoza substantially copied this passage into his famous *History of China*[3] (discreetly suppressing details of the miraculous act of healing), the legend of Miao-shan for the first time took its place in the Western picture of China, a place which, despite its uncertain background and literary credentials, it has continued to hold in the nineteenth and twentieth centuries.[4]

Western scholarly interest in this story has been characteristically bound up with the long-standing search for origins of the Chinese female Avalokiteśvara — a search still in progress and still awaiting a satisfactory conclusion. There has been no serious attempt to clarify the origins and growth of the story itself. The subject has been considered with absurd credulity and with casual scepticism,[5] but Western scholarship has cast little or no light upon it. In China and Japan a number of documented studies have traced the story to its earliest appearances and identified some of its characteristic versions. But here

Introduction

too the traditional focus of attention has been the question of the female Kuan-yin in China.[6]

The present work does not seek to extend the discussion of that well-worn and obstinate problem. It attempts rather to show that, although not the best known of Chinese popular legends, the story of Miao-shan deserves close study in its own right, and for various reasons. It can be traced virtually to the very day of its first appearance before the Chinese public, and its growth from that point on can be followed through a succession of written versions in a wide range of popular forms. It thus offers a unique opportunity to examine how in the traditional Chinese world a story could be shaped and modified in response to the interests and preoccupations of different parts of society. It also appears that the Miao-shan legend was not an isolated or random phenomenon, but stood in a clear relationship to other important legends and themes in the Chinese religious tradition. Study of these matters takes us deep into the corpus of popular writings which span the uncertain boundaries between religion, literature and entertainment: stories, plays, liturgies and ballads which, important or not in themselves, often articulate for us the mythological and ritual themes more dimly implied in conscious literary creations.

This study therefore undertakes the following tasks: to give an account, based on new evidence, of the background and early history of the Miao-shan story from the eleventh to the fourteenth centuries; to discuss versions of the story in later centuries which have not previously received any detailed attention, and to point out certain patterns of relationship; to examine the story's source material, its pattern of development and its range of social and literary contexts; to propose, finally, an interpretation which seeks to integrate these elements into a single framework.

2 The Kuan-yin cult at Hsiang-shan ssu

1. *The monastery and Chiang Chih-ch'i*

IN THE EARLY DAYS of the year 1100 Chiang Chih-ch'i (1031—1104), statesman, administrator and academician of the Northern Sung dynasty, was transferred to the prefecture of Ju-chou, near what is now Lin-ju in southern Honan. It was a temporary demotion in the wake of a political setback in the capital, and Chiang remained at the post for a mere month or less before being moved on to another.[7] During his brief period of office he still found time to visit a Buddhist monastery in his territory, and from this visit there stemmed the first presentation of Miao-shan and her story to the Chinese world. The significance of Chiang's experience and of its short- and long-term effects emerges more clearly when we examine its immediate context.

On a small range of hills known locally as Lung-shan or Huo-chu shan, some few miles to the south-east of the county seat Pao-feng hsien within the Ju-chou territory, there stood a sacred building known as the 'Ta-pei Pagoda'. The term 'Ta-pei' carried a specific reference: it was the name of that Tantric representation of the bodhisattva Kuan-yin with a thousand arms and eyes which had been introduced to China in the early years of the T'ang dynasty and had come to dominate the cult and iconography of Kuan-yin for the next three or four hundred years.[8] There was indeed such a statue at this site, and it is likely, although no documentary source says so explicitly, that it was housed in the pagoda.[9] Later sources claim that the pagoda was built during the T'ang; Kobayashi has also suggested that the bodhisattva image itself, viewed in the context of the spreading cult of Ta-pei in China, may well have been built in the late eighth or early ninth century.[10] But these claims remain undocumented, and it is only in the eleventh century that signs appear of the Ta-pei Pagoda as an object of devout attention.

Among the locally preserved inscriptions on stone which were selectively transcribed in the 1797 edition of *Pao-feng hsien-chih* is one dating from 1051, commemorating the life and works of Chung-hai, a respected local monk.[11] We learn that as a young man from a farming family near Lo-yang he was converted to Buddhism and was attracted to these parts by hearing that 'on Lung-shan, south of the Ju (River), there was an ancient monument popularly known as the "Ta-pei pagoda of Hsiang-shan" '. It is our earliest available reference to the Hsiang-shan site, which was eventually to become a major pilgrimage centre.[12] Chung-hai in fact entered not this monastery but another, situated (according to the local gazetteers) ten *li* to the east of it, or forty *li* to the east of the Pao-feng county seat.[13] Admitted to the order in 1039, he succeeded to the abbot's position when his master died and devoted the rest of his life to the restoring of the old monastic buildings there. By the time of his death in 1051 the monastery had gained the name Tz'u-shou yüan, granted by the emperor Jen-tsung (r. 1023–1063) at the request of a distinguished incumbent of the local prefecture Ju-chou. By the year 1115, however, the monastery had another name, 'Po-ch'üeh ssu', carved on a stone column before the main hall, and the same title reappeared on a monk's memorial stele dated 1311. The new name remained in effect until recent times, and was to play an important role in the later story of Miao-shan.[14] We can only assume that this final change fell late in the eleventh or early in the twelfth century.

During the same critical period the Hsiang-shan monastery itself, with its venerable Ta-pei Pagoda, underwent an important restoration. Later sources fix the year at 1068.[15] A contemporary inscription, transcribed from a stone original in the Hsiang-shan ssu, recorded the special restoration of the Ta-pei Pagoda by a pious donor and his wife in the year 1071.[16] Of the monastic establishment previously attached to the Hsiang-shan ssu we know nothing. The fact of restoration seems to imply the organising initiative of a resident community, but we have to wait until the year 1100 for clearer signs of its activities.

It was at this period of awakening interest and development in the local monasteries that the Hsiang-shan image of Ta-pei came to the notice of Li Chien (1059—1109), writer, connoisseur and devoted follower of Su Shih, who was to leave clear testimony to the artistic excellence of this sacred statue. In his book *Hua-p'in* he described a painting of the Ta-pei Kuan-yin by a ninth-century artist, Fan Ch'iung.[17] He compared the firm, steady balance of Fan's miniature figure, with its many arms, to 'the statue made in person by a human manifestation of Ta-pei at Hsiang-shan in Ju-chou, and the painting done by a human manifestation of Ta-pei at Tung-chin in Hsiang-yang'.[18] As the eleventh century passes into the twelfth, we thus find Li Chien familiar both with the Hsiang-shan statue as a superlative work of art and with a tradition which saw in it the very handiwork of Ta-pei manifest in human form.

Against this background of popular piety and growing monastic activity centred around a sacred image of reputedly supernatural workmanship, one can understand the curiosity felt by Chiang Chih-ch'i when he was transferred to Ju-chou. His experience there is best described in his own enthusiastic words:

> The Thousand-armed and Thousand-eyed Ta-pei Bodhisattva of Hsiang-shan was a human manifestation of Kuan-yin. How wonderful!
>
> In the second year of Yüan-fu, on the last day of the eleventh month,[19] I moved to a provincial post as prefect of Ju-chou. Hsiang-shan in fact lies within the bounds of this administration. The abbot, one *śramaṇa* Huai-chou, sent an acolyte to invite me to the monastery. He accommodated me in the main sleeping quarters and entertained me with vegetarian food. He was earnest and punctilious in his courtesies. Choosing a suitable moment, he calmly said:
>
>> 'On the first day of this month a *bhikṣu* entered the monastery. His appearance and demeanour were most strange, his monk's apparel was in rags. When I asked him, he said that he lived on Chung-nan shan near Ch'ang-an. He had heard that there was a Ta-pei Bodhisattva on Hsiang-shan and had accordingly come to see it and pay reverence.

I then led him in and gave him accommodation. All that night the monk circumambulated (*) the pagoda, stopping when dawn came. Then he came to the abbot's quarters and said to me:

"I once found a book-scroll in a pile of scriptures in an old chamber of the Ling-kan ssu at Nan-shan. The book was entitled *Life of the Ta-pei Bodhisattva of Hsiang-shan*, and it contained the sacred and wonderful words communicated by a divine spirit (天神) in response to the questions of Tao-hsüan, the T'ang Lü Master of Nan-shan. It recounted how the Bodhisattva graciously took on human form. I kept it for a number of years, and later heard that the Hsiang-shan in Ju-chou, Ching-hsi province, is the place where the Bodhisattva attained enlightenment. So I made the difficult journey to come here, hoping to be able to see and pay reverence. And the holy traces are indeed here." Then he took out the *Life* to show me. I thought to myself: "I have long been the abbot of this monastery, and although I wanted to find this story I have never yet got hold of it. Now this monk has actually brought it here. It must be fated." I then made a copy to transmit the text, and the next day when I had finished I wanted to call in the monk to speak with me, but nowhere could he be found. I thought: "Night is already here, where can that monk have gone?" and gave orders to follow him, but no-one knew where he had gone. I do not even know if he was human (*) or divine.'

He then gave me the *Life* to read. It was most detailed, but the language was occasionally vulgar — perhaps because I-ch'ang lacked literary refinement and so missed the original words of the divine spirit. But when it came to the Bodhisattva's own words, they were quite unique — utterances that penetrated the deepest truth.

The Bodhisattva was thus manifest on Hsiang-shan, though as yet no stele records the event. And now I have chanced upon the original story. This must surely be an (*) instruction from the Bodhisattva, desiring me to compose the

---

(*) Each asterisk here and below indicates a character illegible in the original inscription and marked as such in the gazetteer.

record! I have therefore put it in order and set it formally in writing, eliminating the vulgar phrases and preserving the true words of the Bodhisattva. O, when the divine spirit said: 'There will be a revival after three hundred years' (後三百年重興), surely that means now! Now!

This passage is in the form of a historian's personal comment (*tsan* 贊) upon the document he is giving to the world: originally it formed part of a stone inscription which gave the text of the *Life* as revised by Chiang Chih-ch'i. The inscription, standing in the Hsiang-shan ssu, was first engraved in the ninth month of the year following Chiang's visit, hence late in 1100. It bore credits to Chiang himself, as author, and to the powerful and notorious Ts'ai Ching (d.1126) as calligrapher. It was later restored, after heavy weathering, by an abbot of the monastery in the summer of 1308.[20] Students of Chinese mythology will deeply regret that the editors of the 1797 gazetteer were interested in this material solely for the light it could throw on the official career of Chiang Chih-ch'i: they saw no point in transcribing the text of the actual *Life*, which displeased them with the 'extravagance' of its language. Since the inscription seems not to be preserved elsewhere we are thus left without it. It will be argued below that a later twelfth-century source may well give us a close idea of the contents of this *Life*. But we do find an early confirmation of the story told above by Chiang Chih-ch'i in the work of Chu Pien (d.1148), who spent a period of several years (from 1127 to 1144) in captivity under the Jurchen rulers of north China. Chu wrote:

> In the days when he was prefect of Ju-chou, Chiang Ying-shu (*tzu* of Chih-ch'i), at the request of Huai-chou, a monk of Hsiang-shan, took for his subject a divine spirit's account of Ta-pei as written down by I-ch'ang, disciple of the T'ang Lü Master, and developed it into a life-story (潤色爲傳). It was recorded that in the past a certain King Chuang 莊 of some unknown country had three daughters, the youngest named Miao-shan 妙善. She gave her arms and eyes to save her father when he was sick. The story is magnificent, but rather at odds with such scriptures as the *Śūraṅgama* (*sūtra*) and the *Ta-pei Kuan-yin* (*ching*).[21] According to the divine spirit's words, Miao-shan took on the form of the Thousand Arms and Eyes and thus appeared to her parents, then at once

reverted to her original shape. In this case the present-day Hsiang-shan would be the place where Ta-pei attained enlightenment, having been born in a royal palace, incarnate in the person of a woman. Now the traditions passed down through scriptures translated by the saints of old certainly do not agree with this. It is scarcely to be wondered at, since Buddhists like to exaggerate and assume spiritual authority. But (Chiang) Chih-ch'i embellished the story for them in the desire to pass on faith to posterity by doing so. He would hardly have done it unthinkingly![22]

Chu Pien gives the clear impression of having seen the inscription by Chiang Chih-ch'i: he reproduces details that fit exactly with the section preserved for us in the 1797 gazetteer, but he adds more from the main text which is lost to us. We are indebted to him for identifying this as the story of Miao-shan, possessing essential features which we shall examine more closely below. His cool, sceptical attitude to the whole thing can reassure us that his report contains no element of pious exaggeration.

2. *The birth of the legend*

FROM the above two documents seen against their earlier context we can draw some conclusions about the birth of this legend. First, it seems clear that the story of Miao-shan and her epiphany on Hsiang-shan was not public knowledge before the year 1100. Hsiang-shan was certainly a Kuan-yin cult site before that date, but its reputation rested upon the pagoda and the statue of Ta-pei, and the only legend referred to was the tradition that Ta-pei himself had executed the work. Secondly, it is equally clear that the story of Miao-shan shown to Chiang Chih-ch'i and revised by him was closely bound up with this same local tradition of the Thousand-armed and Thousand-eyed Kuan-yin. Chiang refers to it explicitly in the first line of his authorial comment, and the abbot Huai-chou describes how his mysterious clerical visitor came to pay reverence to the Ta-pei pagoda in which the sacred image probably stood. Chiang's own words are strangely chosen. He describes the Hsiang-shan Kuan-yin as a 'human manifestation' of the Bodhisattva, and these ambiguous words oblige us to see a double reference: the statue itself is invested with a sacred identity, but the story of Miao-shan, as we see it reflected in Chu Pien's words, assures us that the girl 'took on the form of the Thousand Arms and Eyes and thus appeared to her parents, then at once reverted to her original shape.' Chiang and Chu both spelled out for their readers the implication that this very hill in the Ju-chou countryside was the site of the Kuan-yin epiphany, but neither attempted to explain exactly what relationship they understood to exist between the girl and the statue. This uneasy tension between sacred image and sacred legend is most clearly revealed when we compare Li Chien's words on the statue with those of Chiang Chih-ch'i: to Li the statue was 'made in person by a human manifestation of Ta-pei' (大悲化身自作); to Chiang, 'the Ta-pei Bodhisattva of Hsiang-shan was a human manifestation of Kuan-yin' (乃觀音化身). The two comments are verbally very close, except that Chiang lacks the vital words '自作', and their absence forces an utterly different interpretation. It is precisely the kind of difficulty that would develop if the story of Miao-shan were being consciously and deliberately brought to bear upon a sacred site which had its own quite distinct background. The verbal smudging of the 'human manifestation' tradition would be one way to suppress or efface the ill fit between these alien partners.

Where did the story actually come from? The inscription offers us a chain of testimony, beginning with the 'divine spirit' in verbal dialogue with Tao-hsüan (596—667), founding father of a branch of the Chinese 'Vinaya' (Lü) sect;[23] their dialogue was recorded, to Chiang's mind none too reliably, by a disciple or scribe, I-ch'ang; the document was then rediscovered centuries later by a mysterious and unnamed *bhikṣu*, who brought it to Hsiang-shan ssu; it was copied by the abbot Huai-chou, who quickly invited the new prefect Chiang Chih-ch'i to see it and hear the accompanying story; Chiang was deeply moved by a sense of historical fulfilment implied in the phrase he quotes from the text — 'there will be a revival after three hundred years' — and took the final step of making the whole story conspicuously public. The enlisting of Ts'ai Ching as calligrapher is a measure of the importance which Chiang attached to his discovery. Although, taken at face value, each element in the chain of testimony depends wholly upon the one preceding it, an act of bad faith by anyone in the line would render everything before him invalid. The earliest elements in the chain thus make the greatest demands on our credulity and are difficult to accept unless they can be confirmed externally. In the case of Tao-hsüan such confirmation is lacking: although he was known for his converse with the divine world and for his collection of sacred traditions concerning Buddhist monasteries, no word of this particular visionary dialogue or of the Hsiang-shan ssu appears in his works on these subjects.[24] The document allegedly found in a pile of scriptures at a Chung-nan shan monastery remains obscure in its origins. The mysterious monk who produces it reveals only enough to associate himself with the 'Tao-hsüan' background, and when he vanishes from the scene we are left openly in doubt as to whether he too is a human or a divine visitor. For all our information down to this point we depend upon the abbot Huai-chou, and for our information on him we depend upon Chiang Chih-ch'i. Of these two the latter gives a greater impression of trustworthiness, if only because he goes out of his way to express puzzled dissatisfaction with the style of the document laid before him. Another characteristic of that document which must leave the detached modern reader uncomfortable is its built-in prediction of a revival 'after three hundred years' — a figure which may not span precisely the lapse in time between Tao-hsüan and Chiang Chih-ch'i, but which certainly struck the latter with the force of a personal summons. It is as if the document had been prepared specially (and successfully) for the benefit of Chiang Chih-ch'i, and by someone whose mastery of literary style did not equal his familiarity with Tao-hsüan's visionary writings.

If these reflections prompt us to look doubtfully at the testimony of Huai-chou, it is logical to ask what he would have stood to gain by devising such a document and giving it such a background. The answer is: a great deal. Tsukamoto Zenryū, without having seen the text of this inscription, has already pointed out that a sacred association with a bodhisattva could bring to a monastery the prestige and economic security of a great pilgrimage centre, the most conspicuous early example being the great complex of Mañjuśrī sites at Wu-t'ai shan in Shansi.[25] We have already noted the restoration and building activities in progress in the monasteries of the 'Hsiang-shan' area during the late eleventh century. Huai-chou, who claimed to be an abbot there of long standing, may well have been involved in this surge of development. If he was now making a bid to turn his monastery into a great centre of pilgrimage by making public the news of Kuan-yin's epiphany, he was destined to be successful on a scale which even he may scarcely have expected. The dramatic story is told in yet another stone inscription from the Hsiang-shan ssu, dated 1185 and recording a restoration of the monastery, by then restyled 'Hsiang-shan Kuan-yin ch'an-yüan'. The text confirms many of the impressions gained from other evidence above, but also supplies the sequel to Chiang's visit:

> Within the bounds of Ju-chou in Honan, below Mount Sung, thirty *li* south of the Ju, there stands on the summit of a hill a Buddhist monastery called Hsiang-shan yüan. It is the holy site where Miao-shan, the youngest daughter of King Miao-chuang-yen 妙莊嚴王 , (* * *).[26] A detailed account of how she appeared in human form (*)[27] is given on an old stone inscription and will not be reproduced here. In the past, from the time of the Sung Yüan-fu reign (1098—1100) on, the abbots of this monastery successively built it up on a magnificent scale and with increasing extravagance. The resident monks numbered more than a thousand. Because the Bodhisattva's relics[28] were there in the pagoda and many miracles were wrought, every spring in the second month[29] people from all parts would come, regardless of distance. The worshippers must have numbered tens of thousands, and they made donations according to their means. The monks of the monastery had no need to go begging to meet their annual budget. They had more than enough ...[30]

The writer refers to the Chiang Chih-ch'i inscription, adding some incidental details to what we already know. But he also shows, by his precise citation of the 'Yüan-fu' date, that this inscription totally transformed the fortunes of the Hsiang-shan ssu, and from his words we can infer an important change in the character of the Kuan-yin cult there. The statue is no longer even mentioned. What attracted the pilgrims, on a scale that raised enough in donations during one month to maintain a thousand or more monks for a year and to put up magnificent new buildings, was the proclaimed presence of relics from the Bodhisattva incarnate, enshrined in the pagoda (*stūpa*), and dispensing miracles to the faithful. The suddenness of this relic-cult, mentioned in no earlier source but now shown to have flourished since the time of Chiang Chih-ch'i's visit, suggests that Chiang's account of Miao-shan's spiritual career on Hsiang-shan carried some reference to the preservation of relics. It also fits well with that sense of new discovery conveyed in the original description of the mysterious *bhikṣu*'s visit: coming expressly to view the site of Miao-shan's epiphany, he recognised the holy presence only after a night of intense contemplation. The relics cannot have been plainly in evidence.

All this tends to reinforce our earlier impression that the copy of the 'Tao-hsüan' scroll shown to Chiang Chih-ch'i by the abbot was shrewdly calculated to awaken a new and fervent popular interest in the Hsiang-shan site. It is an impression that relies on circumstantial evidence, not documentary proof, but it leaves us very reluctant to accept without question the claim of an early T'ang origin for the 'Miao-shan' story. Even in the early twelfth century the same sceptical impulse apparently lurked in the mind of Chu Pien, who expressed his sense of embarrassment at Chiang Chih-ch'i's credulity. Later writers are divided between those who like Hu Ying-lin (1551—1602) scorn the whole thing as monkish fabrication, and others like Yü Cheng-hsieh who are willing to grant the tale some currency in the T'ang; most recently Tsukamoto Zenryū has ventured to demythologise the tradition of the story's creation.[31] No-one since the time of Chu Pien has critically studied the inscriptions cited above. Our re-examination of them suggests two reasons for treating the year 1100 as a starting-point in time for the 'Miao-shan' legend: not only does the alleged earlier background appear open to suspicion, but more importantly, it is clear that before this date the story had made no public impact, locally or at large. Only now did it become a force in Chinese life.

With the new cult thus magnificently launched, the two local monasteries, Hsiang-shan ssu and Po-ch'üeh ssu, now embarked on the long and seemingly inevitable cycle of prosperity, setback and restoration which kept their fortunes alive until recent times.[32] From this point on we are no longer immediately concerned with their history, except to observe in closing that the Po-ch'üeh ssu, which seems to have been at first only tangentially involved in the 'Hsiang-shan' developments, became integrated into the story of Miao-shan and drew much gain from the devout public's undying interest in it.[33]

3 Versions of the story to 1500

1. *The idea of a written tradition*
A STORY which spreads news of a holy site also spreads news of itself. As the legend of Miao-shan created overnight a vast following for the Hsiang-shan ssu, so it also took on a life of its own. The remaining and major part of this book will be concerned with that legend, a new presence in Chinese life, as it spread and developed through the centuries.[34]

It must be made clear at once that this study is based on written versions, in manuscript and published form. I am by no means suggesting, however, that the texts which remain available for our study, or indeed written versions in general, represent a complete and inclusive corpus, encapsulating Chinese experience of the legend. On the contrary, it is clear that the story moved about the land at many levels, through many media. It was transmitted by such very different people as the detached but scrupulous Chu Pien, conscious of an intellectual obligation to his scholarly colleagues, and the village folk who passed on their highly specialised oral versions to Sawada Mizuho in the Hopei countryside of 1941.[35] Between these extremes came authors of fiction and drama, printers of popular ballads, teams of performing evangelists, groups of actors, puppeteers, public singers and storytellers: all with their own aims and motives in recreating for those around them a well-tested story. In what follows we shall look more closely at various different forms of transmission, since it is an axiom of this study that any formulation of a story takes shape within a context, and its interpretation should both draw upon that context and in turn illuminate it. But in an age when anthropologists and folklorists pursue with growing intensity the study of mythology and legend from oral tradition, the return to written texts calls for explanation. What claims can a text-based study make, and to what limitations is it subject?

The answers in this case begin to come when we look at the texts as a group and find that, in terms of their narrative content, they possess a coherence which enables them to be seen as elements in a continuing tradition. Each new re-creation in writing was certainly shaped by its own unique set of particular circumstances, but one central and dominating circumstance common to all appears to have been the pervasive presence of a tradition in writing, however diffuse and imperfectly preserved for us. Although in this area of Chinese literature the notion of textual integrity is so imprecise that to search for specific influences would often be futile, the surviving versions do relate to one another in ways which suggest patterns of influence. There is thus a sense in which the written tradition appears to form a whole of its own and as such to invite study in its own terms. But it does not follow that the written versions existed in abstraction from the life around them. The most important and influential among them were precisely those designed as publications for mass distribution, and their survival in circulation through many centuries is one of the most significant factors to be reckoned with when we begin to form conclusions about the tradition as a whole.

Popular printed books in China could often find their way to a public of awesome dimensions in time and space. Their undeniable importance lay in their normative force extending widely but unevenly through the whole spread of society, and in their simultaneous reflection of values and preoccupations common to the public at large, as they strove for the appeal which would guarantee their circulation and survival. No doubt each publication was designed for its own kind of readership, and our first task must always be to identify each characteristic situation and make allowances for the particular local influences generated in it. But an extended sequence of written sources obliges us to take a more general view: to see a tradition sustained through a long period of time, over a wide geographical area, penetrating many layers of society. A study based on such a view is at a polar extreme from the sampling of testimony in a limited situation. Defining its context on a massive scale, it must eventually set aside the countless immediate and variable particulars through which local phenomena present themselves to the observer. It will aim at the recognition of broad and basic themes.

The legend of Miao-shan presents an unusually apt and interesting subject for such a study: the written versions cover a full progression from specific local situation to universal dissemination. Beginning in the privacy of the abbot's room at Hsiang-shan ssu in January 1100, we follow the story eventually to publication in the most accessible and popular forms.

2. *The version by Tsu-hsiu*

THE *Lung-hsing Fo-chiao pien-nien t'ung-lun*, a chronicle of Buddhist tradition in China from A.D. 64 to 957, was written by Tsu-hsiu, a monk of Lung-hsing fu (the present Nan-ch'ang), in the year 1164.[36] Under his entry for the year 667, recording the death of Tao-hsüan, he included what now represents the earliest connected account of the 'Miao-shan' story available to us.[37] Tsukamoto Zenryū has already suggested that Tsu-hsiu's text may be close to that penned by Chiang Chih-ch'i, basing his impression on the literary quality of the text.[38] Now, with the new material introduced above, we can examine in greater detail how close that correspondence may be. A full translation of Tsu-hsiu's account is given later in this section, but we shall begin here with some particular points of comparison:

Local Material	Tsu-hsiu
words communicated by a divine spirit in response to the questions of Tao-hsüan, the T'ang Lü master of Nan-shan (*Chiang inscription, 7b*)	Tao-hsüan, Lü Master of Nan-shan, ... once asked a divine spirit about the history of the Bodhisattva Kuan-yin. The spirit replied: ...
a certain King Chuang of some unknown country (*Chu Pien*)	There was a king whose name was Chuang-yen (*name of his country not given*)
King Miao-chuang-yen (*1185 inscription, 4b*)	
three daughters, the youngest	she bore him three daughters,

Versions of the story to 1500

named Miao-shan (*Chu Pien*)	the eldest Miao-yen, the second Miao-yin, the youngest Miao-shan.
Miao-shan, the youngest daughter (*1185 inscription, 4b*)	
The Bodhisattva severed and cast away the bonds of affection, and gladly followed the True Way (*1185 inscription, 5b*)	'I prefer to retire to pursue a life of religion... In all the emotional entanglements of this world there is no term of spiritual release.'
she gave her arms and eyes to save her father when he was sick (*Chu Pien*)	the king contracted jaundice... she gladly gouged out her eyes and severed her arms...
Miao-shan took on the form of the Thousand Arms and Eyes and thus appeared to her parents, then at once reverted to her original shape (*Chu Pien*)	And then the holy manifestation of the Thousand Arms and Thousand Eyes was revealed... In a moment, the Bodhisattva reverted to her former person.
the Bodhisattva's relics were there in the pagoda (*1185 inscription, 4b*)	the king, the queen and the two sisters made a funeral pyre, preserved the holy relics and on that same mountain they built a *stūpa*.
'I... heard that this Hsiang-shan in Ju-chou... is the place where the Bodhisattva attained enlightenment.' (*Chiang inscription, 7b*)	'Hsiang-shan is pre-eminent. The mountain lies 200 *li* to the south of Mount Sung. It is the same as the Hsiang-shan in present-day Ju-chou.'
The present-day Hsiang-shan would be the place where Ta-pei attained enlightenment (*Chu Pien*)	
Within the bounds of Ju-chou, below Mount Sung... there is a Buddhist monastery called	

Hsiang-shan yüan. It is the
holy site where Miao-shan, the
youngest daughter of King
Miao-chuang-yen, (* * *).
(*1185 inscription, 4b*)

The material in the left-hand column does not represent direct quotation from Chiang Chih-ch'i's original, but reflects certain of its features through the words of intermediaries. (In two cases, of course, Chiang himself is an intermediary, commenting on his own text.) Exact verbal parallels cannot be expected.

The parallels that do emerge range from the relatively predictable (Miao-shan as the third and youngest daughter), which hardly vary in any version of the story, to the highly specific (the relics in the *stūpa* on Hsiang-shan). The movement of the story as a whole seems to proceed in each case along identical lines, with one substantial exception: three of the 'local' sources insist upon the enlightenment of Miao-shan on the mountain, an important development never openly introduced by Tsu-hsiu. His account of the story can be read as implying the enlightenment, but the absence of a phrase so strongly echoed elsewhere suggests that here at least Tsu-hsiu has rephrased the story, not transcribed it mechanically. He has also failed to reproduce the utterance of the divine spirit which is explicitly quoted in the inscriptions: 'The traces left on earth by a holy one are subject to rise and fall in their fortunes; there will be a revival after three hundred years' (1185 inscription, 6ab; Chiang, 8a). This is clear proof that the text of Tsu-hsiu is not a complete verbatim reproduction of the 1100 inscription. At the very least he has edited it slightly, conceivably he has rewritten it completely.

There are, however, equally clear signs that this version was written with some reference to the Chiang original. The very fact that it is presented in the form of Tao-hsüan's dialogue with the spirit shows that Tsu-hsiu did not meet the story at large and out of context: he is here quite faithful to the detail of the original. Far more importantly, he brings out the intimate connection of the story with the Hsiang-shan ssu in Ju-chou. Three essential features remain intact in his account: the fleeting manifestation of the Thousand Arms and Eyes

Versions of the story to 1500

(immediately evocative of the long-standing 'Ta-pei' tradition at the monastery); the preservation of the Bodhisattva's relics in a special *stūpa* (the very heart of the twelfth-century cult there); and the careful geographical pinpointing of the site, following the spirit's deliberate emphasis of its supreme importance. Of these three, the last most overwhelmingly recalls the sceptical view first voiced by Chu Pien and restated above. Such phrasing is precisely what we would expect to find in a document designed to promote a cult at a particular monastery: it is indeed echoed in all three 'local' sources, and the businesslike inclusion of the relics and their *stūpa* only serves to reinforce the impression that a vigorous local interest is being canvassed. These details were the first to dwindle and disappear in the general currency of the story, which lived on without need of the cult at Hsiang-shan ssu. It was suggested above (ch. 2.2) that the sudden appearance of a relic cult at the monastery implied some reference to the relics in Chiang's inscription. Tsu-hsiu gives us precisely that. Internal evidence thus suggests that Tsu-hsiu's version reflects the contents of Chiang Chih-ch'i's lost text, although some editorial distance clearly separates them.

The evidence is enriched, and the suggestion strengthened, by a passage in a much later source, an annotated version of the popular *Vajracchedikā* commentary *Chin-kang k'o-i* 金剛科儀. At a point where this text alludes to Miao-shan's refusal to take a husband, the editor Chüeh-lien (whose preface is dated 1551) supplies a gloss giving a detailed account of the whole story.[39] His version, late though it is, corresponds remarkably closely to what we have from Tsu-hsiu's pen. The similarity is obvious but by no means straightforward. For this reason the two versions are here translated in parallel, so that precise comparisons can be made more easily.

Tsu-hsiu

[277b] Ch'ien-feng, second year, eighth month: Tao-hsüan, Lü Master of Nan-shan, died . . .

Chüeh-lien

[129a] Miao-shan refused to take a husband, and most certainly achieved buddhahood. *[Note follows:]*

Once in the past the Lü Master [Tao-]hsüan dwelt in the Ling-kan ssu in the Chung-

The Master once asked a divine spirit 天神 about the history of the Bodhisattva Kuan-yin.

The spirit replied:

'In a past age there was a king whose name was Chuang-yen 莊嚴. His lady was named Pao-ying 寶應. She bore three daughters, the eldest Miao-yen 妙顏, the second Miao-yin 妙音, the youngest Miao-shan 妙善.

At the time of Miao-shan's conception the queen dreamed that she swallowed the moon. When the time came for the child to be born [-278a] the whole earth quaked, wonderful fragrance and heavenly flowers were spread near and

nan mountains, practising religion. In a vision a *deva* 天人 attended him. The Master asked the *deva*: 'I have heard that the Mahāsattva Kuan-yin has many links and manifestations on Sahā, this earth. In what place are they most abundant?'

The *deva* replied: 'The Bodhisattva's appearances follow no fixed rule, but the pre-eminent site of his bodily manifestation is Hsiang-shan.'

The Master enquired: 'Where is this 'Hsiang-shan' now?'

The deva replied: 'Over two hundred *li* to the south of Mount Sung there are three hills in a row. The middle one is Hsiang-shan — that is the Bodhisattva's place. To the north-east of the hill there was in the past a king whose name was King Miao-chuang-yen [主=王]. His lady was named Pao-te 寶德. The king had no crown prince, only three daughters: the eldest Miao-yen 妙顏, the second Miao-yin 妙音, the youngest Miao-shan 妙善. Of these three daughters two were already married.

Versions of the story to 1500

far. The people of that country were astounded. At birth she was clean and fresh without being washed. Her holy marks were noble and majestic, her body was covered over with many-coloured clouds. The people said that these were signs of the incarnation of a holy person. Although the parents thought this extraordinary, their hearts were corrupt, and so they detested her.

As she grew up the Bodhisattva became naturally kind and gentle. She dressed plainly and ate only once a day.

Only the third, in conduct and appearance far transcending the ordinary, always wore dirty clothes and took but one meal a day, never eating strongly flavoured food, and pursued this life of abstention and religious discipline without faltering in her resolve.

In the palace she was known as 'the maiden with the heart of a Buddha'. By her good grace the ladies in waiting were converted: all turned to the good life and renounced their desires.

The king took some exception to this and prepared to find her a husband.

The king said to Miao-shan: [-129b] 'You are no longer a child now — you ought to take a husband.'

Miao-shan, with integrity and wisdom, said: 'Riches and honour are not there for ever, glory and splendour are like mere bubbles or illusions. Even if you force me to do base menial work, I will never

Miao-shan said: "The river of desire has mighty waves, the sea of suffering has fathomless depths. I would never, for the sake of one lifetime of glory, plunge into aeons of misery. I earnestly repent [of my resolve].'

When the king and his lady sent for her and tried to coax her, she said: 'I will obey your august command if it will prevent three misfortunes.'

The king asked 'What do you mean by "three misfortunes"?'

She said: 'The first is this: when the men of this world are young their face is as fair as the jade-like moon, but when they grow old their hair turns white, their face is wrinkled; in motion or repose they are in every way worse off than when they were young. The second is this: a man's limbs may be lusty and vigorous, he may step as lithely as if flying through the air, but when suddenly an illness befalls him he lies in bed without a single pleasure in life. The third is this: a man may have a great assembly of relatives, may be surrounded by his nearest and dearest, but suddenly one day it all comes to an end [with his death]: although father and son are close kin they cannot take one another's place. If it can prevent these three misfortunes, then you will win my consent to a marriage. If not, I prefer to retire to pursue a life of religion. When one gains full understanding of desire to leave my home and pursue the way of religion.'

Versions of the story to 1500

the Original Mind, all misfortunes of their own accord cease to exist.'

The king was angry. He forced her to work at gardening and reduced her food and drink.

Even her two sisters went privately to make her change her mind, but Miao-shan held firm and would not turn back.

The queen personally admonished her.

Miao-shan said: 'In all the emotional entanglements of this world there is no term of spiritual release. If close kin are united, they must inevitably be sundered and scattered. Rest at ease, Mother. Luckily you have my two sisters to care for you. Do not be concerned about Miao-shan.'

The queen and the two sisters therefore asked the king to release her to follow a religious calling.

The king was angry. He called for the nuns.

He charged them to treat her so harshly that she would change her mind. The nuns were intimidated, and gave her the heaviest tasks to do — fetching wood and water, working with pestle and mor-

The king angrily cast her out into the flower garden at the rear of the palace, cut off her food and drink, and made her mother strongly urge her to take a husband.

Miao-shan said: 'Empty things come to an end — I desire what is infinite.'

Furious at hearing this, the king summoned Hui-chen 惠真, a nun of the White Sparrow monastery 白雀寺, to take her off to the monastery to grow vegetables, and to devise ways to induce her to return to the palace.

tar, running the kitchen garden. In response to her, the vegetables flourished even in winter, a spring welled up beside the kitchen.

Much time went by, and Miao-shan still held firm to her purpose.

The king heard about the miracles of the vegetables and the spring of water, and was furious. He sent soldiers to bring back her head and to kill the nuns.

As they were arriving, mountains of cloud and fog suddenly appeared, totally obscuring everything. When it cleared, Miao-shan was the one person they could not find.

She had been borne off by a spirit (神) to a crag in another place, there to live. The spirit then said: 'The land here is too barren to sustain existence.' He moved her altogether three times before they reached the present [令 = 今] Hsiang-shan.

Miao-shan said: 'Surely you have heard that those who obstruct someone's monastic vocation will suffer torments [芒 = 苦] for countless aeons? Do you dare oppose the best interests of the Buddhist religion and willingly accept the retribution of hell?'

The nun answered: 'I am under the king's orders. This is nothing to do with me.'

Miao-shan would not consent. She remained firm in her desire to enter the order.

The nun reported it to the king, who in a great rage ordered troops to surround the monastery, behead the nuns and burn down their quarters.

Miao-shan was taken off by a *nāga* spirit (龍神)

to the foot of Hsiang-shan, not a hair of her injured.

Versions of the story to 1500

Miao-shan dwelt there, eating from the trees, drinking from the streams.

Time went by, and the king contracted jaundice (*kāmalā*). His whole body was corrupt and suppurating, he could no longer sleep or feed.

None of the doctors in the country were able to cure him.

He was about to die when a monk appeared, saying he was well able to cure him,

but would need the arms and eyes of one free of anger.

The king found this proposal extremely difficult to meet.

The monk said: 'On Hsiang-shan, in the south-west of Your Majesty's dominion, there is a bodhisattva engaged in religious practices.

If you send a messenger to present your request to her you can count on obtaining the two things.'

She built a hut and lived there, clothed in grass and eating from the trees, unrecognised by anyone.

Three years had passed by when the king, in return for his crimes of destroying a monastery and killing the religious, contracted jaundice (*kāmalā*) and could find no rest.

Doctors could not cure him.

He advertised far and wide for someone to make him well.

At that point a strange monk appeared, saying: 'I have a divine remedy which can cure Your Majesty's sickness.'

The king asked: 'What medicine do you have?'

The monk said: 'If you use the arms and eyes of one free of anger to blend into a medicine and take it, then you will be cured.'

The king said: 'This medicine is hard to find.'

The monk said: 'No, it is not. There is a Hsiang-shan in the south-west of Your Majesty's dominion, and on the very peak of the hill is a holy one (仙人) whose practice of religion has come to completion. This person has no anger. If you put your request to her she will certainly make the gift.'

The king had no choice but to command a palace equerry to go and convey his message.

Miao-shan said: 'My father showed disrespect to the Three Treasures, he persecuted and suppressed the True Doctrine, he executed innocent nuns. This called for retribution.'

Then she gladly cut out her eyes and severed her arms. Giving them to the envoy, she added instructions to exhort the king to turn towards the good, no longer to be deluded by false doctrines.

When the two things were submitted to him the monk made them up into medicine. the king took it and instantly recovered. He generously rewarded the monk-physician. But the monk said: 'Why thank me? You should be thanking the one who provided the arms and eyes.' Suddenly he was gone. The king was startled by this divine intervention.

Ordering a coach, he went with his lady and two daughters to the hills to thank

The king ordered an equerry to take incense into the hills and bow to the holy one, saying: 'Our lord the king is sick. We venture to trouble you with a request for your arms and eyes in order to save the king's life. This will lead him to turn his mind to enlightenment.'

Hearing this, the holy one gouged out her two eyes and severed both arms with a knife, handing them over to the equerry.

At that moment, the whole earth shook. The equerry returned to the capital.

There they made the monk blend the medicine. The king took it and recovered from his sickness.

In solemn procession the king then went to Hsiang-shan, where he offered humble

Versions of the story to 1500

the bodhisattva.

They met, and before words were spoken the queen already recognised her: it was Miao-shan. They found themselves choking with tears.

Miao-shan said: 'Does My Lady remember Miao-shan? Mindful of my father's love, I have repaid him with my arms and eyes.'

Hearing her words, the king and queen embraced her, bitterly weeping.

The queen was about to lick the eyes with her tongue, but before she could do so, auspicious clouds enclosed all around, divine musicians began to play, the earth shook, flowers rained down. And then the holy manifestation of the Thousand Arms and Thousand Eyes was revealed, hovering majestically in the air.

thanks and veneration.

He saw the holy one with no arms or eyes, physically defective. The king and his lady, looking from either side, were deeply moved to a painful thought: 'The holy one looks very like our daughter.'

The holy one said: 'I am indeed Miao-shan. Your daughter has offered her arms and eyes to repay her father's love.'

Hearing her words, the king embraced her with loud weeping. He said: 'I was so evil that I have made my daughter suffer terrible pain.'

The holy one said: 'I suffer no pain. Having yielded up my mortal eyes I shall receive diamond eyes; having given up my human arms I shall receive golden-coloured arms. If my vow is true these results will certainly follow.'

Heaven and earth then shook. And then the holy one was revealed as the All-merciful Bodhisattva Kuan-shih-yin of the Thousand Arms and Thousand Eyes, solemn and majestic in form, radiant with dazzling light, lofty and magnificent, like the moon amid the stars.

Attendants numbered tens of thousands, voices celebrating [the bodhisattva's] compassion resounded to shake the mountains and valleys.

The king and [於 = 與] his lady, together with the entire population of the land, conceived goodness in their hearts and committed themselves to the Three Treasures.

In a moment, the Bodhisattva reverted to her former person, then with great solemnity departed.

The Bodhisattva then entered *samādhi* and, perfectly upright, entered *nirvāṇa*.

The king, the queen and the two [-278b] sisters made a funeral pyre, preserved the holy relics and on that same mountain they built a *stūpa*.

[Tao-]hsüan again asked: 'The Bodhisattva can take mortal form in any place, and surely ought not to be present solely at Hsiang-shan.'

The spirit replied: 'Of all sites at present within the bounds of China Hsiang-shan is pre-eminent. The mountain lies two hundred *li* to the south of Mount Sung. It is the same as the Hsiang-shan in present-day Ju-chou.'

Broadly speaking, two things are at once clear when we set these two accounts side by side: first, that they present an identical narrative sequence with almost complete consistency; second, that they share very little verbal text in common. Each is explicit about different aspects of the story. While Tsu-hsiu dwells upon the miraculous conception and birth of Miao-shan, sets out at length her defiant speech to her father and carefully reports her tribulations in the monastery, Chüeh-lien is more scrupulous in recording proper names and resorts more frequently to direct speech. Between the two versions there is much complementary give and take of incidental detail, but at virtually no point is there any collision or inconsistency: they could easily blend into a single harmonious narrative.[40] Their distinctive wording, however, shows clearly that we are not dealing with a simple case of copying. We have to think instead of some common source which each editor has reproduced or paraphrased in his own way. Elements shared by both versions probably derive from that original, and a striking number of small details fall into this category. The conversation of Tao-hsüan with his divine informant; the geographical pinpointing of the Hsiang-shan site, and of the kingdom to its north-east[41] where Miao-shan was born; the names of the characters, which differ only in the expansion of the king's own name to Miao-chuang-yen (as we found it in the 1185 inscription), and in part of the queen's name (see note 40); the 'jaundice' (kāmalā 迦摩羅) which afflicts the king in both versions; the 'freedom from anger' required in the donor of the arms and eyes; the circumstances of the revelation of the Thousand Arms and Eyes: these are only the most conspicuous points in a dense body of shared narrative detail.

The 1551 Chüeh-lien version, though separated by several hundred years from the events in twelfth-century Pao-feng, shows an intimacy of relationship with Tsu-hsiu's version of 1164 which illuminates some of the uncertainties we have considered above. We find that, although Chüeh-lien cuts his story short at the end of Miao-shan's life and adds nothing about the preservation of her relics, he does make it clear that she first entered *samādhi* and *nirvāṇa*, and thus supplies the one detail that seemed conspicuously lacking in Tsu-hsiu's version when compared with the local sources (cf. table above). He, like Tsu-hsiu, fails to reproduce any reference to a 'revival after 300 years', but he does include in the story a local feature that was conspicuously absent in Tsu-hsiu's work — the name of the monastery where Miao-shan served as a hard-worked novice. It is the Po-ch'üeh ssu, whose fortunes ran parallel with those of the neighbouring Hsiang-shan ssu in the eleventh and twelfth centuries (cf. above, chapter 2). Although Tsu-hsiu leaves this monastery unnamed, it by no means follows that Chiang Chih-ch'i did so too. The Po-ch'üeh ssu is named at this point in the story in all other versions early and late, and its appearance in a source which seems so close to the local traditions of the early Hsiang-shan legend points to its presence in the original inscription.

Tsu-hsiu and Chüeh-lien were almost four centuries apart in time. We do not know their actual sources of information on the Hsiang-shan legend — whether they consulted the inscription of 1100 *in situ*, saw it reproduced in rubbings or transcriptions, or used other sources reflecting its contents more indirectly. They have, however, left us two complementary accounts of the legend which, taken together, seem to stand closer than any other known version to the original source. In the discussion below, this will be our starting point.

3. Thirteenth-century references

WE consider here not connected versions of the story but reflections which confirm that, in the century following the Hsiang-shan revival and the first reporting of the story in written form, it remained in continuing currency.

The first is in a Buddhist work, the *Ts'ung-jung lu*, in which Hsing-hsiu (1156—1236, or 1166—1246) amplified and commented on the theses and *dicta* of a predecessor in the Ch'an tradition, Cheng-chüeh (1091—1157).[42] In a section devoted to the Kuan-yin of the Thousand Arms and Eyes we find the brief remark: 'I have seen it claimed that Ta-pei was once the Princess Miao-shan — this was told to the Lü Master (Tao-)hsüan by a divine being.' The argument goes on to point out that the Bodhisattva could be manifest in innumerable ways: this was just one of any number of possible appearances (4.261c). The form of the allusion, beginning with Ta-pei and then introducing the human identity, exactly matches the approach in Chiang Chih-ch'i's own original comment. The appearance of Tao-hsüan and his divine informant obviously echoes it too.

Hsing-hsiu, who spent his career mostly in major cities in north China, may or may not have seen the Hsiang-shan inscriptions for himself, but he seems at least to have known the legend in a form not too far removed from the local source.

The second allusion appears in the *Hsin-pien Tsui-weng t'an-lu* by Chin Ying-chih. The work is known to students of fiction as an early popular collection of items of narrative interest. It cannot be exactly dated, but its text contains no date later than the early thirteenth century.[43] Part of the collection deals with Buddhist matters, and one item there concerns the use of money given for the carving of sacred images. The opening words at once introduce the Kuan-yin of the Thousand Arms and Eyes, who 'attained enlightenment on Hsiang-shan, was manifest in the Southern Sea; showing great mercy delivered all beings from their sufferings; giving her arms and eyes [repaid] the debt of love to the king her father.'[44] There follows some encouragement to devotion, and the passage then proceeds to the matter of carving statues.

Here at one stroke we are far from the world of Buddhist orthodoxy. We witness instead a picture in miniature of what Kuan-yin represented to the devout public at large. The brief phrases no longer convey a sense of narrative sequence: they assemble various salient characteristics of Kuan-yin piety into a single composite impression. The transformation implied here is fundamental. It is not simply that the Hsiang-shan story was now well known in lay tradition, but that it had already become part of the standard Kuan-yin mythology, standing shoulder by shoulder with other classic popular attributes. More than this, the citation of the story brings out themes which will develop increasing importance in later treatments. Its outstanding points of interest are seen to be the resolute princess's successful quest for enlightenment on Hsiang-shan, and the supreme filial response to parental love implied in her sacrifice of arms and eyes. This tiny allusion in fact exemplifies for us a principle of thematic selection and development which will become the main subject of our concluding chapter below. Juxtaposed with the remarks of Hsing-hsiu above, it displays the transition from a documented revelation, specific in its geographical reference and cultic significance, to a legend of catholic appeal, drawing its strength from the values of personal piety.

There is another strange but unmistakable reflection of the

legend in a source surviving in printed editions usually dated to the thirteenth century: the *Ta-T'ang San-tsang ch'ü-ching shih-hua*.[45] This unique work, famous as an early version of the story which later established itself as the *Hsi-yu chi*, takes the T'ang pilgrim Hsüan-tsang ('Tripitaka') through a series of mythical episodes on his historic but by now completely fictionalised journey to India. The brief opening section, missing from both extant editions, is followed by two in which the pilgrim encounters first the celestial monkey Hou hsing-che who is to be his guide and support, then the powerful tutelary deity Mahābrahmā Devarāja (identified with Vaiśravaṇa, the Buddhist King of the North). Thus protected he ventures out to face the unknown. And at this precise point he comes to Hsiang-shan:

> They set out on their winding way and came to a mountain whose name was Hsiang-shan. It was the place of the Bodhisattva of the Thousand Arms and Eyes, and also the place where the Bodhisattva Mañjuśrī pursued his mental cultivation. Raising their heads, they saw the inscribed name: 'The Monastery of Hsiang-shan'.

It is not a reassuring place. Tripitaka is terrified by the menacing guardian figures at the gate and downcast by the monastery's deserted buildings. His monkey companion now grimly warns him that the road ahead is devoid of human contact, roamed by tigers, wolves, snakes and hares; signs of human habitation are all illusions wrought by sorcery. Tripitaka gazes around him with a smile of resignation, then pursues his way.[46]

The Master Tripitaka's visit to this very monastery at the outset of his journey into the wilds raises large questions which will call for extensive discussion on another occasion. What interests us here is that Hsiang-shan is now a clear and familiar landmark on a holy journey. Its connection with the Ta-pei Kuan-yin is explicit, but the local details give way to a blurred composite image in which Mañjuśrī also now appears, and the physical surroundings serve a specific purpose in the context of Tripitaka's journey.[47] It is as though, in this early and unpretentious specimen of printed fiction, the Hsiang-shan legend were already familiar to the point of vagueness.

4. *The version by Kuan Tao-sheng*

YÜ Cheng-hsieh's formidably erudite study of the female Kuan-yin, dated 17 September 1803, takes the form of a postface to a piece entitled *Short Life of the Bodhisattva Kuan-shih-yin* (*Kuan-shih-yin p'u-sa chuan-lüeh* 觀世音菩薩傳略).[48] He describes it as printed from the calligraphy of Kuan Tao-sheng (1262—1319), wife of the famous painter and calligrapher Chao Meng-fu (1254—1322), the work being executed in 1306. Copies of the original print, unknown today, were apparently also rare in the nineteenth century: when Yü Yüeh (1821—1907) first referred to it in his notebooks he knew it only from Yü Cheng-hsieh's testimony; later he reported having seen the text, but certain details betray that it was not the original.[49] It seems surprising that none of the modern Japanese scholars writing on this subject appear to have gained access to the text of Kuan Tao-sheng's version, which was in fact reprinted in the *Lü-ch'uang nü-shih*, a compilation partly devoted to literary work by women authors, available now only in late-Ming editions.[50] The title of Kuan Tao-sheng's text is given as *Life of the Mahāsattva Kuan-yin* (觀音大士傳), and the authorship is credited to 'Lady Kuan' 管夫人 of the Yüan. No date is appended. It is, however, beyond doubt textually the same as the version studied by Yü Cheng-hsieh. His references to the text are brief and condensed, but they do reflect characteristics of phrasing which answer closely to the text in *Lü-ch'uang nü-shih*: in some cases it is even possible to correct imperfections in the latter by reference to Yü.[51] He appears therefore to have used a good print, perhaps the original, and there is no reason to doubt the 1306 date he reports.

Kuan Tao-sheng was an excellent calligrapher. On one occasion the emperor commissioned a piece of work from her for preservation 'so that later ages will know that there were fine women calligraphers under our Dynasty.' She was a devout Buddhist, and 'wrote by hand scores of copies of the *Vajracchedikā*, which she presented to famous monasteries and famous monks.' This we have on the authority of her husband, writing at the time of her death.[52] His words lend complete credibility to Yü Cheng-hsieh's report and enable us to define a precise context for the *Short Life*. It was evidently written out as an aristocratic devotional exercise, printed, not perhaps for common meritorious distribution (as with truly popular religious texts), but more likely for the circulation of presentation copies in high monastic society.

This tells us little about the background to the text Lady Kuan used as her model. Its title significantly employs the term *lüeh* 略, which suggests abridgement, and the account indeed reads like a summary of some more extended treatment:

> [1a] Kuan-yin was born in the West with the name Miao-shan, the youngest daughter of King Miao-chuang. From her childhood she abstained from meat and kept the precepts of religion. She was naturally inclined to the simple and plain and possessed outstanding intelligence and wisdom. As they came to marriageable age, the king sought husbands for his daughters. The two eldest, Miao-yin and Miao-yüan, obeyed him. But Kuan-yin, because she defied the king, was disgraced. The king reduced her food and clothing. He commanded his ladies to urge her to obey, but she would not. In anger, the king cast her away to the White Sparrow Monastery (Po-ch'üeh ssu), instructing the abbess to compel her obedience. He allowed a space of seven days at the end of which, failing a satisfactory report, all the nuns in the monastery would be burned to death. The terrified nuns drove her about her tasks like a slave, but Kuan-yin kept to her resolve more firmly than ever. With her own hands she did the heavy kitchen work, just as if spirits were toiling on her behalf. The abbess fearfully reported this to the king, who said that it was all lies and had the monastery surrounded and set alight. Five hundred nuns were burned up without trace. Only Kuan-[1b]yin sat erect, reciting *sūtras*, and the flames could not harm her.
>
> The king then sent for her and lectured her on what was and was not good for her, in the hope that she would change her mind. But Kuan-yin said: 'The old don't grow young again, the dead don't return to life. The cycle of life and death is endless suffering. Your daughter withdraws from pomp and splendour simply because she wishes to live for ever.' The king's wrath grew when he heard this reply. He commanded her to be taken to the place of execution to suffer the penalty. But just as she was to be beheaded, the sword of its own accord broke in two, and a tiger roared on to the execution ground and bore away Kuan-yin on its back.

The king assumed that she died in the tiger's jaws.

The tiger carried Kuan-yin along for a thousand *li*, then set her down in a forest. At first she remained unconscious. She dreamed that two boys in black led her on a tour of Feng-tu, the Underworld. She met the one they call Yama, who received and attended her with the greatest respect. She also saw all the sinners, dismembered, burned, pounded and ground up, receiving their fill of suffering. Then Kuan-yin recited *sūtras* on their behalf, so that they were delivered.

When she awoke, the venomous dragons and evil beasts of the forest were struggling to pursue and bite her. Kuan-yin was ill at ease in this place. Suddenly, as she was taking refuge in a hermitage, an old [2a] man gave her mountain peaches to eat and conducted her to Hsiang-shan, where she made her dwelling. These surroundings were secluded and peaceful, unsullied by any worldly impurity. Here Kuan-yin pursued religious cultivation for some years, and people believed that all enlightenment and religious fulfilment resided in this place.

One day, sitting in her cell, Kuan-yin saw from afar that the king was sick and foul, close to death. He had advertised with gold for a doctor, but none had responded. She then magically took the form of an aged monk and reported to the throne that the king could be healed only by the arms and eyes of his closest kin. The king regarded his two daughters as his closest kin, but when he sent for what he needed from them neither daughter obeyed the command. The king again asked the monk's advice. He said: 'A holy elder on Hsiang-shan works the salvation of living beings. There you will certainly get what you need as soon as you ask.'

The king sent envoys to seek this favour from the holy elder, who then severed her own two arms and cut out her two eyes, handing them to the envoys to take back for the monk to mix into a physic. The king took it and recovered. In great delight he honoured the monk with a high office and rich rewards. The monk would not accept them. He simply said: 'The holy elder has performed a great service for you. You must go tomorrow and offer your thanks in person.'

[2b] The king agreed. He quickly took his carriage and hastened on his way. When he met the holy elder, she was indeed without arms or eyes and her body was covered in

streams of blood. The king was grieved, and also startled to find her appearance so closely resembling Kuan-yin — she must be his third daughter Miao-shan. He humbly besought heaven and earth to make her whole again. In a short while the holy elder had arms and eyes by the thousand [巳 = 以]. And then Kuan-yin bowed before him, and to their utter delight they expressed to one another the feelings proper to father and child. She urged him to practise good works, and he did so, cleansing his mind and changing his ways, so that finally she was able to soar aloft together with the king.

Kuan-yin ascended to the Western Paradise and entered the assembly of Buddhas. She keeps perpetually open the gate of deliverance from suffering, she points out to all the way to the highest destiny, she observes the cries of all the world in times present and past, she discerns the good and evil throughout the society of men. This is the reason for her title 'Kuan-shih-yin'.[53]

This narrative is explicit but functional, and lacks the eloquence of Tsu-hsiu's version, with its dramatic use of dialogue and powerful sense of climax. Here, by contrast, such effects are muted. A more subtle difference stems from the formulation of Lady Kuan's text as a document of Kuan-yin piety. Her narrative suffers a certain flatness from the persistent use of the name 'Kuan-yin' throughout, whereas Tsu-hsiu, although often introducing the word 'bodhisattva', allows the girl to keep her secular name right to the moment of her transfiguration in the form of the Thousand Arms and Eyes. The heightened sense of revelation is lost in the Kuan version, which goes on to close with a paragraph of conventional piety.

We cannot know whether this text, adopted for calligraphic, not literary, purposes, would have stood the test of general circulation. But regardless of its specific literary character, the version of Kuan Tao-sheng reproduces a story which has undergone radical change from what we knew hitherto. It has lost the relics and the *stūpa*, and presents in their place an apotheosis in which the reconciled father and daughter ascend aloft. It also loses the Hsiang-shan monastery, but still specifies the Po-ch'üeh ssu as the place where Miao-shan endured her early monastic trials. (This detail, although absent from Tsu-hsiu's account, may well have been part of the body of local reference in the original inscription by Chiang Chih-ch'i — see above, section 2.) The major innovation, however, is a remarkable central section inserted into the narrative after Miao-shan's rescue from the threatened nunnery. She provokes her father to the point of sentencing her to death; a tiger bears her away unharmed to a forest, where in a dream she visits Hell and intercedes for the damned; only then, awaking, is she escorted to Hsiang-shan, where the original story resumes.

It is difficult not to see this as an episode separately introduced into the original story. It is absent in Tsu-hsiu's version, and there the sensitive passage proceeds so smoothly that one cannot easily imagine it masking some drastic editorial stroke which has eliminated a long central section:

> He sent soldiers... As they were arriving, mountains of cloud and fog suddenly appeared, totally obscuring everything. When it cleared, Miao-shan was the one person they could not find. She had been borne off by a spirit to a crag in another place, there to live.

The same rescue, a little differently phrased, takes place in the version by Chüeh-lien, and it is not easy to guess why both he and Tsu-hsiu would have wanted to suppress such a central section, if there had been one in the original. The obvious inference is that Kuan Tao-sheng's early fourteenth-century account represents a revised version of the story into which the execution scene and the visit to Hell have been introduced. We cannot say whether such a version would be a recent revision or a parallel tradition of some standing. But certainly the new episode assumes an importance which makes it an integral part of all other known versions from this point on. In particular it is characteristic of the *pao-chüan* tradition described immediately below, which has roots leading back almost to the very source of the Miao-shan legend in the early twelfth century.

The full implications of this new episode can be explored only in a discussion of the anatomy and interpretation of the story, in later chapters. But here we can at least recognise in Lady Kuan's pious exercise the earliest datable example of the Miao-shan legend in its standard popular form.

5. *The early growth of a 'pao-chüan' tradition*

AS used by modern scholars, the term '*pao-chüan*' covers a corpus of popular texts written largely in a characteristic mixture of prose with verse for chanting or singing. The extant and datable pieces span a period from the late fifteenth century to modern times. The corpus includes liturgical and homiletic texts, stories and other works on religious themes and, in more recent centuries, treatments of standard popular tales. Studies by Chinese and Japanese specialists supplemented by reports by Western observers have progressively revealed the close relationship of *pao-chüan* literature to the teachings and social values of a loose, but pervasive and enduring system of minority religious sects in traditional China.[54] Deriving elements of their philosophy, mythology and liturgy from the recognised traditions of Buddhism and Taoism, the sects were stigmatised as 'heterodox teachings' 邪教 by spokesmen of the established intellectual and religious systems. They nevertheless played a continuing part, sometimes violent and usually concealed, in the life and history of China from the Sung dynasty down to recent times. The teachings and activities of the sectarian religions in later centuries have been extensively studied elsewhere[55] and must be briefly returned to below. What concerns us here is the sustained presence of organised devotional activity at a popular level from the very period when the Hsiang-shan story first issued from its source.[56] It was against this broad background that the earliest known *pao-chüan* were to emerge, and we can accept that the proselytising and group teaching work of the popular sects provided a medium in which such stories could be spread and exploited for their religious and social impact.[57]

There are signs that the Hsiang-shan story was indeed put to such use from an early period. Popular devotional texts from the twelfth and thirteenth centuries refer to Kuan-yin as the princess who would not take a husband.[58] An actual title, '*Hsiang-shan chüan*', appears in one of the earliest lists of *pao-chüan* to come down to modern times — in the *Wei-wei pu-tung T'ai-shan shen-ken chieh-kuo pao-chüan* 巍巍不動泰山深根結果寶卷.[59] But in spite of this circumstantial testimony no early text remains. As Li Shih-yü has pointed out, the early sects operated secretly and no doubt circulated their texts in manuscripts now scarcely surviving at all.[60] Much later, in the eighteenth, nineteenth and early twentieth centuries, when the printing of *pao-chüan* had become widespread at a popular level, a large quantity of *pao-chüan* literature on the Hsiang-shan theme was in circulation, now represented by many preserved editions. Scholars have sought to bridge the critical gap in time by postulating a continuity of tradition: certain of the late editions are held to derive from early origins.

One in particular has been singled out as representing a direct tradition from the thirteenth or fourteenth centuries. It is in the collection of Yoshioka Yoshitoyo, who has done the world of scholarship the service of reprinting it in full in reduced facsimile.[61] Its title as given on the first page of text is *Kuan-yin p'u-sa pen-hsing ching* 觀世音菩薩本行經, while the short form *Hsiang-shan chüan* appears on the fold of each folio. The first page also lists out the names of four Buddhist masters responsible for the composition, circulation, revision and transcription of the text — P'u-ming, Pao-feng, Chih-kung and Wen-kung. The first two of these played a part more closely described in the opening pages. P'u-ming, a monk of the Upper T'ien-chu monastery near Hangchow,[62] is said to have been sitting alone on 17 September 1103 when he received a visitation from a monk who urged him to further the work of universal salvation through the story of Kuan-yin. P'u-ming listened to his recitation, wrote it up as a text, then witnessed a vision of Kuan-yin with the classic attributes, Pure Vase and Green Willow, in her hand (2b—3a). At some unspecified later time Pao-feng, in retreat on Lu-shan in Kiangsi, had P'u-ming's text laid before him by a 'female *mahāsattva*' 女大士. She urged him in turn to make this aid to salvation widely available to those spiritually too immature to discover the truth through the methods of Ch'an. Pao-feng wrote out ten copies (1b—2a).

The edition in the Yoshioka collection bears the date 1773 and the name of the Chao-ch'ing ssu in Hangchow (130b).[63] Despite the huge lapse of time separating it from the visionary experience of P'u-ming it still represents the earliest dated *Hsiang-shan pao-chüan* known to us and the only recorded copy from the eighteenth century.[64] Yoshioka regards it as more authoritative than any other previously used and suggests, from internal evidence, that it preserves features of a very early version, standing in a 'direct tradition from the Yüan edition'.[65] But we must modify these enthusiastic claims in the light of some further observations.

1. The 1773 text is by no means as unique as Yoshioka's introduction represents. It is indistinguishable in title, preface, pagination, lineation and textual detail from other much later editions of the *Hsiang-shan pao-chüan*, two of which I have studied in British libraries.[66] Further comparison might well reveal that holdings elsewhere belong to the same family of editions. The Yoshioka text should be seen more realistically as the earliest known representative of this not uncommon textual family.

2. Yoshioka seeks to explain the words '*pen-hsing ching*' of this title and the '*pen-hsing ching chien-chi*' 本行經簡集 of titles in later reprints[67] by reference to the early versions of Chiang Chih-ch'i and Kuan Tao-sheng. But our study of the new material introduced above makes it clear that there can be no question of discernible textual relationships. What we know of Chiang's version differs in detail from the present text, and Kuan Tao-sheng has bequeathed a short version too rigorously and uniformly adapted to reveal any textual characteristics of its original model.

3. The internal dating of the text is impressionistic at best. Yoshioka uses a point of linguistic evidence to link it to the Yüan era — the plural suffix written 每 .[68] This is certainly found in vernacular sources of the Yüan period, but by no means only there. The late sixteenth-century *Chin P'ing Mei tz'u-hua* abounds in examples of the same graphic usage.[69] There are, moreover, some unambiguous signs that the text of the 'Yoshioka' edition must at least have undergone revision in the Ming or Ch'ing periods. It twice uses the title *hsü-pan* 序班 to designate palace functionaries who superintend the contact of court personnel with the emperor (12a, 49b); and it once also uses the title *ming-tsan* 明讚 (*sic*) (49b). Both were first introduced under the Ming dynasty and continued by the Ch'ing, and their functions were broadly as we find them represented in the *Hsiang-shan pao-chüan*.[70] There can thus be no question of claiming the simple authority of a Yüan text in what we have here.

A more realistic view of the *Hsiang-shan pao-chüan* system represented by Yoshioka's edition does not detract from its value and interest. Although as a text it cannot be regarded as an integral survival from an early period, it clearly belongs to a long-standing tradition of *pao-chüan* treatments of the Hsiang-shan story. Such a tradition no doubt had its own areas of free development: Sawada Mizuho has shown, for instance, how the recitations of *pao-chüan* represented in the *Chin P'ing Mei* often differed widely from textual versions available to us.[71] But a connected tradition may also possess its own form of narrative integrity. If, from the jumble of surviving *pao-chüan* on the 'Miao-shan' theme,[72] we select the present text for discussion in our 'pre-1500' category, it is primarily because of its remarkable internal pedigree. The supernatural overtones of P'u-ming's experience, and later that of Pao-feng, were calculated to add to the work's authority in the minds of its readers. From our detached standpoint they may have the opposite effect, but we cannot fail to be struck by the precision of the date on which P'u-ming allegedly first heard the story in his Hangchow monastery. Although P'u-ming remains otherwise unknown to us, we do know that at that very point in time Chiang Chih-ch'i was prefect of Hangchow. He had regained political favour at the accession of Hui-tsung and was eventually appointed to Hangchow on 23 November 1102. He was not replaced in this office until 31 October 1103, some weeks after P'u-ming is said to have received the story on 17 September.[73] In the historical half-light of *pao-chüan* studies such a coincidence of dates is irresistible. It is certainly plausible enough to visualise Chiang Chih-ch'i, with the recent Ju-chou experience fresh in his memory, visiting the Kuan-yin centre under his new official charge and bringing with him the sacred communication from the north. Since the *Hsiang-shan pao-chüan* records this 1103 date without reference to Chiang Chih-ch'i, we cannot reasonably suspect the interference of some antiquarian hand, retrospectively filling in historical data. What emerges is rather a sense of internal preservation through a tradition. It is this hint of a broad continuity reaching back to the first years of the legend's circulation that brings the eighteenth-century *Hsiang-shan pao-chüan* into our discussion of the early period.

The text is on a much larger scale than any so far discussed. It covers 130 folios. The bulk of the narrative proceeds through alternating passages of prose and of loosely rhyming verse in seven-syllable rhythm. There is no use of the ten-syllable line familiar in other *pao-chüan*, but the work opens and closes with sections in which the verse interludes take the form of five- and ten-syllable lines grouped in a pattern styled '*gāthās*' (1a—9b,

127a—130b). The prose is in a simple and wooden literary idiom dominated by a four-syllable rhythm, with occasional lapses into colloquialism.

The passages of verse serve at times to further the narrative, at times pause to elaborate descriptively on the implications of the prose. Scattered couplets of a reflective or descriptive nature punctuate the narrative irregularly, marked off by circles at the head of the column. Also distributed through the text are one-line invocations to Kuan-yin which have the effect of saturating the whole work in an aura of religious devotion and of adding intensity at key moments, when the narrative forces its way breathlessly through many such pious interjections.[74]

In its broad lines the treatment of the story is remarkable for following the sequence sketched out in 1306 by Kuan Tao-sheng. There are differences of detail, but they have no significant effect on the progress of the story. Three examples will illustrate the point:

1. The burning of Po-ch'üeh ssu.

This is the monastery in which Miao-shan first submits to the hardships of monastic discipline and which incurs the royal displeasure. In the Kuan version it is burned down around her ears and the inmates all die. The *Hsiang-chan pao-chüan* has it initially saved by Miao-shan's prayers (51a—52a); but although the nuns are spared immediate death by fire, she later asks in Hell for the deliverance of some who died 'of fright' on that occasion (73a); then in due course she hears that the king her father has vindictively burned down the monastery and killed the inhabitants (86a).

2. Miao-shan's visit to Hell.

In the version of Kuan Tao-sheng the visit is technically a dream experience, since Miao-shan has been rescued alive from the executioner's hands and laid down unconscious in a forest. In the *pao-chüan* the reader is more sharply confronted with the full reality of execution: the princess, though at first protected by Kuan-yin's own protective power over weapons of execution,[75] voluntarily accepts death by strangulation, and it is her dead body that the tiger bears into the Forest of Corpses (67b—69b). Her tour of Hell and later revival thus take her more clearly across the frontiers of life and death. As she sets out for Hsiang-shan she is as before offered a magic peach by an old man (82a). But it is only after nine years of meditation

there that she first receives the name 'Kuan-yin' in the body of the narrative (85b).
3. The closing scene of the story.
The *pao-chüan* preserves the transfiguration (but with only a vague allusion to the Thousand Arms and Eyes: 118b), and differs from the Kuan version only in that the father lives out his life, dies at the age of eighty-nine, and has his cremated remains preserved in a *stūpa* (121a).

The *pao-chüan* preserves certain details found in our earliest source, the version of Tsu-hsiu, supplemented by that of Chüeh-lien: the king's disease is still called *kāmalā* (87a), and the gift of arms and eyes is still required from one 'free of anger' (93a). But in this expansive treatment of the story the inherited framework supports a mass of minor circumstantial detail. Many particulars are interesting for their occasional reflections of ritual and mythology, but also for their attempt to rationalise the vague, alien setting of the original story in more comprehensible Chinese terms. The king presides over the full panoply of a Chinese imperial court. He has a named state to rule (Hsing-lin), a reign-title (Miao-chuang), a family name and a personal name (P'o Ch'ieh). This is just one of several efforts made in different versions to force the Sanskrit-based names of the original story inelegantly into Chinese forms. The place-names betray the same uneasy encounter of mythical and real, alien and familiar. Although the land of Hsing-lin is said to lie in a world to the west of Mount Sumeru (3a), it somehow overlaps with China: Miao-shan asks to go to the Po-ch'üeh *ch'an* monastery of Lung-shu hsien in Ju-chou (37a); her later journey to Hsiang-shan is long and difficult — it lies in Ch'eng-hsin hsien, part of the Hui-chou territory (80b). Imaginary Buddhist names are thus cheerfully set in real Chinese contexts.[76] By now, of course, the true situations of Ju-chou, Hsiang-shan and the Po-ch'üeh ssu are of no concern to author or reader, nor were they in the version reproduced by Kuan Tao-sheng. The story has established its own identity: the tangible data once so essential in its original context now submit to a new set of priorities.

In the *Hsiang-shan pao-chüan* these priorities impose themselves conspicuously in the substance of the narrative. The simple story gains in size and weight but loses its pace and drama. This is because the text pauses to explore with infinite care the emotional and religious implications of each new scene. In the first half of the story, ending with Miao-shan's execution, the effect is of a series of incidents (the refusal to marry — the punishment in the palace garden — the entry to the threatened monastery — the return to the palace) punctuating an endless, agonised dialogue between Miao-shan and her baffled family. In the *pao-chüan* it is of supreme importance that the story should openly and fully spell out the conflict between monastic and family ideals. As Miao-shan is approached in turn by her father, mother, sisters and others in the palace, as she is punished, threatened, lured with all the means at the king's disposal, each aspect of her intolerable but unshakable decision is examined at length. This extended homily is balanced symmetrically by pages near the end of the work in which the members of her family stand before the disfigured Miao-shan while the implications of her action and sacrifice sink home to them. She then addresses to each some moralising remarks, which ensure that the force of the story's events is not passed by.

In sum, the *Hsiang-shan pao-chüan* that we know in eighteenth and nineteenth-century editions gives a clear and convincing idea of how and why the story of Miao-shan was adopted in early *pao-chüan* tradition. Cut loose from its specific local origins, the story now invited attention as a text of Kuan-yin piety in the broadest sense, but also as a document in which the painful conflict of religious ideals with family loyalties could find an authentic resolution. In this sense the *pao-chüan* presents itself as a teaching text, and its apparatus of religious terminology and commentary, sometimes with sectarian overtones,[77] finds its justification in that end. The survival of this tradition into modern times, constantly reprinted and circulated by pious donation,[78] is itself an expression of the Chinese public's reaction.

4 The sixteenth and seventeenth centuries

AFTER THIS LONG PERIOD of concealed transmission — an extended progress irregularly glimpsed in scattered sources and inferred as a submerged *pao-chüan* tradition — the story reappears in the sixteenth century, now in full illumination. Historians of Chinese fiction and drama have long recognised in the sixteenth and seventeenth centuries a period of incomparable fertility and activity both in the development of vernacular literary forms, and in the production of books for a wide public readership. The legend of Miao-shan was one of many traditional themes now adapted and brought before the reading public in popular and accessible literary forms. The evidence which now remains from this period enables us to study the story as it was most widely and enduringly disseminated. Some of the publications of the period have remained in print until recent times, and their influence can be detected in various quarters. They show the narrative content of the story gaining in petty circumstance, taking on some features of the age and its preconceptions, but in its essentials remaining true to the pattern already established.

1. *The 'Nan-hai Kuan-yin ch'üan-chuan'*

THESE characteristics are well represented in a short novel dating probably from the late sixteenth century and still found in circulation within the last hundred years.[79] Editions of the *Nan-hai Kuan-yin ch'üan-chuan* 南海觀音全傳 are briefly described by Sun K'ai-ti, Liu Hsiu-yeh and Liu Ts'un-yan.[80] The latter two reports concern an edition in the British Library which represents the only known text likely to antedate the nineteenth century. The remarks which follow refer to it specifically.

Publication details are as follows:
Title page: Entitled *Ch'üan-hsiang Kuan-yin ch'u-shen nan-yu chi chuan* 全像觀音出身南遊記傳.

Title in text: Hsin-ch'ieh ch'üan-hsiang Nan-hai Kuan-shih-yin p'u-sa ch'u-shen hsiu-hsing chuan 新鍥全相南海觀世音菩薩出身修行傳.[81]

Division: 4 *chüan.* The narrative is divided into 25 headed sections (listed, but with several inaccuracies by Liu Ts'un-yan, pp. 216—7); most, not all, are marked by a large circle above the heading. They are not styled *hui* 回.

Lineation: 10 columns, 17 characters.

Printed area: 19.0 x 12.5 cm.

Illustrations: At the top of each page, flanked by four-word captions. The title-page has a slightly larger illustration, without caption, in the same position. A full-page picture of Kuan-yin ends the work on 4.18b.

Compiler/editor: Two names appear on the first page of *chüan* 1: 'Hsi-ta wu-ch'en tsou-jen' of Nan-chou 南州西大午辰走人 and Ch'ung-huai Chu Ting-ch'en of Yang-ch'eng (Canton) 羊城冲懷朱鼎臣. Their work is described as 'editing' 訂者 and 'compiling' (編輯) respectively. A certain amount is known about the activities of Chu Ting-ch'en, who was associated in a similar capacity with five other extant texts from the late sixteenth century.[82]

Publisher: The title-page names a publishing house, the Huan-wen t'ang 煥文堂, which is noted elsewhere as issuing a short anonymous novel of the Ch'ing period.[83] But it is by no means certain that this title-page was integral with the original blocks from which the edition was printed, and indeed the quality of its illustration does not seem consistent with those in the text. A printer is named on 1.1a — T'ai-chai Yang Ch'un-jung of Hun-ch'eng 渾城泰齋楊春榮. He may have been related to the well-known Yang publishers of Chien-yang, Fukien.[84]

Extent: Complete. Pages 2.17b, 2.19b and 3.14b are repositioned out of order.

The book stands squarely within a class of popular fiction

issued by a group of Chien-yang publishers during the course of the Wan-li reign (1573—1619). This can be shown by comparison with a group of thirteen specimens chosen from a much larger range of similar publications for their specially close resemblance to the *Kuan-yin* work. Identified by short titles, they are:

1. *Chung K'uei ch'üan-chuan* 鍾馗全傳
2. *Ch'eng-yün chuan* 承運傳
3. *Niu-lang Chih-nü chuan* 牛郎織女傳
4. *Hsüan-ti ch'u-shen chuan* 玄帝出身傳
5. *Hua-kuang t'ien-wang chuan* 華光天王傳
6. *Ta-mo ch'u-shen ch'uan-teng chuan* 達摩出身傳燈傳
7. *Shang-tung pa-hsien chuan* 上洞八仙傳
8. *T'ang San-tsang hsi-yu shih-o chuan* 唐三藏西遊釋厄傳
9. *Nien-ssu tsun te-tao lo-han chuan* 廿四尊得道羅漢傳
10. *Huang-Ming chu-ssu kung-an chuan* 皇明諸司公案傳
11. *Ming-ching kung-an chuan* 明鏡公案傳
12. *Hsiang-ch'ing kung-an* 詳情公案
13. *San-tsang ch'u-shen chuan* 三藏出身傳 [85]

All items on this list have a virtually certain, usually identifiable, Chien-yang provenance. The *Nan-hai Kuan-yin ch'üan-chuan* shares with them the following characteristics:—

[items 1—13] identical treatment of illustrations, placed at the top of each page and flanked by short captions; division into *chüan* and headed sections, not listed *hui*;

[items 1—12] identical style of lineation: 10 columns, 17 characters (item 13 differs only in having 19, not 17, characters to the column);

[items 1—6, 13] division into four *chüan*;

[items 1, 2, 7] prefacing of the text with an introductory verse set to a specified tune (a convention borrowed from the *ch'uan-ch'i* drama of the Ming period); item 1 employs the same tune as the *Kuan-yin* work.[86]

The various established publishing families of Chien-yang represented here were presumably in competition with one another, and we can hardly describe this group of books as a 'series' in the modern sense. Yet there is a marked degree of uniformity, and it extends beyond bibliographical features. Items 10—12 are collections of crime-case stories, item 2 a short historical novel, but items 1, 3—9 and 13 all draw their subject-matter from traditional religious legend and can be broadly described as fictionalised lives of gods and saints. The *Nan-hai Kuan-yin ch'üan-chuan* belongs clearly within this large latter group. One other item in the same group — no. 8, a version of the *Hsi-yu chi* — was compiled by the same man, Chu Ting-ch'en. It has been the most closely studied of the six publications associated with his name. I have elsewhere argued from textual evidence that Chu based this work in part on an early edition of the recently-published *Hsi-yu chi* in 100 chapters, in part on another abridged version of it (no. 13 above).[87] Other views have since been expressed concerning Chu's specific sources, but no attempt has been made to question the view advanced in 1969 that he was essentially an adapter of established publications.[88] He worked in an unsophisticated medium, without much technical polish or sense of literary decorum, casual in orthography, unashamedly popular in its range of reference. The presentation of the narrative, in its short, easily digested sections, each wound up with a trim verse quatrain or couplet, the unbroken flow of simply labelled illustrations — all this was designed for readers seeking light, undemanding entertainment.

Unlike the *Hsi-yu chi* adaptation, in which the nature of his sources seems to have led the editor into difficulties of proportion and consistency, the present *Kuan-yin* work presents a homogeneous appearance. But the story is now garnished with much material designed to add to its narrative interest and fill out its incidental circumstance. The result has made it diffuse and in places absurd. What we now read is a novelette of adventure which preserves little of the earlier striving for a serious and devout response. Not only has its texture been densely filled out with named accessory characters — ministers, generals, palace maidens, and the like — but its design has been complicated by a series of episodic sub-plots of varying importance. Thus — the three royal sisters enter the story as reincarnations of three sons of a devout *gṛhapati* family, whose celestial adventures are laid before the reader while King Miao-chuang awaits a response to his prayers for offspring. Later in the story, when the sick king sends envoys to Hsiang-shan, his two sons-in-law, who from the start have treated him with disrespect, plot his assassination and are foiled by the supernatural intervention of Miao-shan; for this they are sentenced to death, and their wives, the royal sisters, confined in the palace, where Miao-shan in a dream converts them to the religious life. Later again, when the king is healed and prepares to set out for Hsiang-shan to give thanks, two beasts guarding the Buddha's gate — a green lion and a white elephant — take on the form of young men, abduct the two imprisoned sisters to a remote mountain and unceremoniously ravish them, then do the same with two palace maidens; they proceed to intercept and kidnap the travelling king and queen, while the throne is usurped by the son of one of the dead sons-in-law; the situation is resolved by a grand celestial battle on lines familiar from the sixteenth-century *Hsi-yu chi* and *Feng-shen yen-i*, and indeed deploying much the same celestial army and arsenal; the king and his party are now freed by Miao-shan, who has been away at a Mid-Autumn party, and return to reclaim their kingdom by force. Only after this fantastic and protracted episode (it occupies nearly a quarter of the whole text) can the royal party proceed to its long-awaited reunion on Hsiang-shan. Miao-shan's own spiritual career has meanwhile been enriched, immediately after her first arrival at Hsiang-shan, by episodes introducing her two disciples Shan-ts'ai and Lung-nü.

All this, superimposed on the powerfully coloured legend we know from older sources, creates an effect of bewildering superficial vividness. It provoked de Groot and others to a dismissive assessment of the legend — 'un vrai tohubohu d'éléments bouddhiques et taoïques'.[89] But such a comment, easy enough to make, fails to illuminate the full range of circumstances concealed behind the book's first confusing impression. Chu Ting-ch'en and his colleague were treating their subject as a story of action and excitement. They were well aware that the episodes listed above were extraneous to the central traditional story: this much is clear from the *Che-ku-t'ien* verse standing at the head of their work, which methodically lists out the stages of the traditional story without any mention of other narrative elements. If in their own version they went on to add new material they no doubt had their own good reasons. They seem to have taken up materials at hand and treated them in a manner which had proved its success with the public.

We cannot point to clear textual sources used in the composition of these new episodes, and perhaps it is beside the point to seek them when the compiler was often simply using the common mythological currency of his time. In introducing Miao-shan's two attendants, for instance, he did no more than provide her with standard attributes of the female Kuan-yin, an iconographical form by now well established in Chinese society.[90] For other contemporary parallels to the introduced material we usually need look no further than the hundred-chapter *Hsi-yu chi* and certain other titles in the 'Chien-yang' group of saints' lives. When Shan-ts'ai is recruited, it is by plunging to his death from the cliffs of P'u-t'o shan and then, spiritually regenerate, seeing his own mortal remains left at the cliff-foot; in a similar scene, Tripitaka is shown his drowned mortal body borne away by the stream which he is crossing to reach Paradise.[91] Lung-nü, the dragon-king's daughter, comes to Miao-shan through the agency of the 'grateful fish', a motif used widely in Chinese fiction and adopted by Chu Ting-ch'en in another episode (the story of Ch'en Kuang-jui and the infant Tripitaka) which he may well be responsible for introducing into the text of the *Hsi-yu chi*.[92] The long adventure with the lion and the elephant has its parallel in a major episode of the *Hsi-yu chi* (chaps. 74–77): the same beasts (together with a third, the Great Roc) abduct Tripitaka on his pious journey and finally submit, after an elaborate struggle, to the figures whom they serve as mounts in standard Buddhist iconography — Mañjuśrī and Samantabhadra.[93] In this *Kuan-yin* book it is apparently necessary for Miao-shan to perform the act of deliverance herself.[94] But although the overt connection with the two 'parent' bodhisattvas is thus suppressed, the text still preserves the site of the beasts' lair on Ch'ing-liang shan, the classic abode of Mañjuśrī but associated elsewhere in Ming fiction with both bodhisattvas jointly.[95] The bodhisattvas themselves emerge belatedly in the final apotheosis as the transfigured forms of the two outraged sisters — and with crude but undeniable justice they then receive the miscreant beasts as their mounts (4.17a).

The process of composition which lay behind the *Nan-hai Kuan-yin ch'üan-chuan* comes more sharply into focus when we see the work stripped of these extraneous episodes. There then remains an account of the Miao-shan story which is recognisably related to the *Hsiang-shan pao-chüan*. The two works share in common the proper names of many places and characters in the story,[96] and they follow the same specific sequence of individual narrative units — a conversation between given characters in one version will be matched, within the limits indicated below, by a similar conversation in the other. There are also many passages of shared text. They are concentrated within the central part of the main narrative, beginning at the point where Miao-shan is first summoned before her father to hear him propose her marriage, and ending with the healing of the sick king. Two breaks in this sequence correspond to episodes already noted above.[97] The shared passages are sporadic but plentiful. They are not limited to prose, but the verse parts of the two texts share little more than occasional phrases, with the exception of one extended passage in which as many as eight lines are substantially the same in both, although differently ordered.[98] The prose parallels between the two texts are far more significant, and on examination they reveal a consistent pattern. Appearing usually in passages of dialogue, formal debate and documentary statements, they show the *Nan-hai Kuan-yin ch'üan-chuan* less enthusiastically eloquent, lacking many phrases found in the *pao-chüan*, but richer in points of petty narrative detail.

Since the sharing falls well short of complete textual identity, we must think in terms of a *rewriting* process, in which the author of one text has had constant recourse to the other in working out the core-narrative of his own version. Various circumstantial reasons for regarding the *pao-chüan* as the prior text have already been noted. There are early references to the existence of such a work. The text we now possess conforms in narrative content to an early traditional pattern which, in Chu Ting-ch'en's version, we find grotesquely distorted, although acknowledged in an opening verse. Specific textual variants between the two versions generally find the Chu text inferior. There are also slips in his narrative consistency of a kind which have been pointed out in his version of the *Hsi-yu chi*.[99] All this makes it seem likely that Chu Ting-ch'en or his editorial colleague sat down to work with a copy of the *Hsiang-shan pao-chüan*, apparently very much as we now know it, as his staple source for a fictional reworking of the Miao-shan legend.

Its lack of conventional fictional incident and its interminable moralistic dialogues, sprawling through long stretches of monotonous verse and prose, must have tried his patience. He reduced the debates to a token length, brought in a rich cast of named supporting characters, and worked into the story whatever ideas he could gather from the current printed fiction dealing with traditional religious figures, and probably from other more ephemeral sources. He used a stylistic format which was standard in his immediate professional milieu and found little place in it for the heavy proportion of narrative verse in his *pao-chüan* source.

Such a reconstruction, though dependent on less intimately related textual evidence and subject to more imponderables, is consistent in kind with two other cases of fictional adaptation in the period c. 1585—1625. One is Chu Ting-ch'en's own work on the *Hsi-yu chi*, in which we see the same focus on action and incident. There too (if my earlier arguments are substantially accepted) he ruthlessly cut down the rich fabric of spoken dialogue and expansive stretches of formal description which are so essential to the success of the hundred-chapter novel, and inserted an action-packed but incongruous episode. Another rather different case has been described more recently: the reworking of the *chantefable* work *Yün-men chuan* 雲門傳 into vernacular short story form, leaving a large proportion of the prose text intact, has been characterised as 'opportunistic adaptation'.[100] Chu Ting-ch'en's treatment of his *chantefable* source was bolder than this, but probably merits the description no less. It is not easy to attribute to him motives of creative integrity.

The *Nan-hai Kuan-yin ch'üan-chuan* emerges from this examination in a poor light. Yet its importance is remarkable and undeniable. In China its pervasive influence can be felt in popular local renderings of the Miao-shan story down to modern times.[101] In the West, largely through the agency of de Groot, it has decisively shaped much thinking and writing about the later cult of Kuan-yin.[102] With this book, as with the *Hsiang-shan pao-chüan*, the legend of Miao-shan indeed arrives at a point of universal dissemination and takes on the principal forms by which it is to be generally known through the last centuries of traditional Chinese life.

2. *Saints' lives in the late Ming*

ANOTHER important source of written diffusion can be traced to this same period. The *Ch'u-hsiang tseng-pu sou-shen chi ta-ch'üan* 出像增補搜神記大全 and the *San-chiao yüan-liu* sheng-ti fo-tsu sou-shen ta-ch'üan 三教源流聖帝佛祖搜神大全 both date from the late Ming. They are illustrated handbooks of pious lore set out as collected lives of gods and saints. In distributing these pantheons nominally among the Three Religions they reflect the fashionable philosophical universalism which coloured works of popular piety in their time.[103] Other such popular pantheons had existed before. One with similar title and contents, the Sou-shen kuang-chi 搜神廣記, said to date from the Yüan period, was listed in the famous collection of Mao Chin (1599—1659),[104] but it does not survive.

The two present works are extant in late Ming editions: the former in what is regarded as a first edition by the Fu-ch'un t'ang of Nanking, with a preface by Lo Mao-teng dated 1593;[105] the latter in several undated editions both early and late, and in a standard modern reprint of 1909 by Yeh Te-hui.[106] The contents of both have been carefully studied by Li Hsien-chang, who suggests that they derive from a common source and that they contain material preserved from Yüan times, much of which was supplemented, deleted or completely revised under the Ming. He prudently concludes that the contents of the two books are best studied item by item.[107]

In both works there is a notice on Kuan-yin, identifying the bodhisattva with Miao-shan and relating her story. The contrast between these two treatments of the story seems consistent with Li Hsien-chang's observations on other items in the two books. The Tseng-pu sou-shen chi presents a spare, economical account in less than two hundred characters, preserving the shape of the classic story told by Kuan Tao-sheng and by the Hsiang-shan pao-chüan.[108] Some proper names and points of detail are at odds with other sources, one (the name of the forest, Shih-to-lin, where Miao-shan's body is brought by the tiger) shared only with the pao-chüan. But there is no problem of consequence here: the Tseng-pu sou-shen chi account stands squarely in a standard tradition. The San-chiao yüan-liu entry, however, is six times as long and much more circumstantial.[109] It is of interest chiefly because, alone among sources for this period, it closely matches the contents of the novelette Nan-hai Kuan-yin ch'üan-chuan. A comparison of proper names shows at once how well these two accounts agree, in contrast to all earlier sources.[110] The same can be seen in the story line as such. The San-chiao yüan-liu introduces its heroine as a reincarnation of Shih Shan, the *gṛhapati's* son. It also takes the king to pray for offspring at the Temple of the Western Peak. Both these introductory episodes we find in the *Nan-hai Kuan-yin ch'üan-chuan*, but in no other early source. Beyond this, there are actual verbal echoes between the two versions. Both explain the assignment of punishments in Hell with a particularity not matched by the *Hsiang-shan pao-chüan*, and sometimes in the same words.[111] Miao-shan's indignant response to the disguised Śākyamuni's tempting proposal of marriage after her return to life contains in both versions a distinctive phrase not to be found in the *pao-chüan*.[112] Both versions award identical Buddhist titles to members of the family in the final apotheosis.[113] Other such parallels could be cited. But the correspondence is still not absolute. The *San-chiao yüan-liu* version contains none of the later episodes found in the *Nan-hai Kuan-yin ch'üan-chuan*: there are no scheming sons-in-law, and the whole story is rapidly wound up in two lines once Miao-shan is established on Hsiang-shan; even the healing of her father is briefly disposed of, and there is no sign of extraneous incident.[114] Certain tiny narrative details also deviate from their equivalents in other versions.[115]

The 'Kuan-yin' entry in *San-chiao yüan-liu* is not alone in its relationship with a work of current fiction. Li Hsien-chang discovered a similar case when he examined the notice on the goddess Ma-tsu and compared it with a short novel, the *T'ien-fei niang-ma chuan* 天妃娘媽傳, printed in the Wan-li period by the Chien-yang publisher Hsiung Lung-feng.[116] It is a work which but for its alleged division into *hui* might have joined the list of 'Chien-yang' saints' lives above. Like the *Kuan-yin* novel it reflects the strong influence of the *Hsi-yu chi*. Here too certain new material introduced into the traditional story is shared by the *San-chiao yüan-liu* and the short novel. The case of Ma-tsu thus seems to present a parallel to that of Miao-shan.

How the *San-chiao yüan-liu* stood in relation to these Fukien novels is not clear. There is no obvious priority in time. Li Hsien-chang indeed associates both *San-chiao yüan-liu* and *T'ien-fei niang-ma chuan* with the year 1592,[117] and Chu Ting-ch'en's *Nan-hai Kuan-yin ch'üan-chuan* could easily have appeared around the same time, since other work by him dates from 1584 and 1591.[118] Any attempt to find the internal relationship between the works also comes down to guesswork:

they may after all have been linked indirectly through other texts unknown to us. We can only judge plausibilities. It seems harder to conceive the *Nan-hai Kuan-yin ch'üan-chuan* as simultaneously under the influence of both *Hsiang-shan pao-chüan* and *San-chiao yüan-liu* than to suppose the latter basically derived from the novel. The simplest possible view is to see the *San-chiao yüan-liu* compiler taking the novel as the main source of his 'Kuan-yin' entry, reducing the opening episodes to their bare essentials, methodically reproducing the texture of incidents and names in the main narrative, concentrating on those parts of greatest interest to readers of pious books (e.g. the visit to Hell), and disregarding the extraneous fictional episodes near the end.

These technical questions must remain open as long as we lack firm dates and remain vulnerable to the host of minor discrepancies which cast doubt on any attempt at internal reconstruction. But the works discussed here certainly offer unanimous testimony to a remarkable surge of creative activity in popular hagiography during the Wan-li period, an activity which in its vigour and long-lasting influence rivals the contemporary achievements in other fields of creative endeavour. The *San-chiao yüan-liu sou-shen ta-ch'üan* has remained in print until recent times and is still cited as a standard source on popular hagiography. Whether its account of the Miao-shan story claims precedence over the contemporary *Kuan-yin* novel or the reverse, the two works between them have brought their version of the story to a widely extended readership in time and space.

3. *First signs of a theatrical tradition*

THUS far the sources present a succession of printed narratives, mostly in simple prose forms, to some extent related among themselves, circulating within their appropriate milieux. They have been treated as a single broad system (admittedly with its areas of irregularity and local variation) in which the development of the story appears as a progression in time. This progression reaches a point of climax in the last years of the sixteenth century: the story takes on a new guise which becomes quickly established and remains conspicuous, even standard, until recent times.

We began, however, by stressing that such an organically

developing written tradition forms only one part of a world of rich cultural activity. The early evidence hints only faintly at the existence of that richer world. It is, once again, only in the late sixteenth century that we see the first clear signs of transmission in forms other than printed narrative. This is a late appearance. But it by no means follows that narrative in print commanded a monopoly or a priority in earlier times. Narrative texts can survive because, granted the right circumstances, books preserve them. Performances survive, if at all, only fleetingly through mutable and vulnerable traditions. Usually no more than echoes remain, caught and preserved at those important moments when, as in the last decades of the Ming period, writers, anthologists and publishers turned their attention to the performing arts and created from them a copious, though imperfectly preserved, literature.

It is from this background that a printed edition of the play *Hsiang-shan chi* 香山記 comes down to us. It was one of a large group of plays in the *ch'uan-ch'i* form issued by the Nanking publishing firm Fu-ch'un t'ang during the Wan-li period.[119] The play has been linked with the name of Lo Mao-teng, whose connection with the Fu-ch'un t'ang has been noted above. It is said to have borne a preface by him dated 1598 and adding the pen-name 'Erh-nan-li-jen' 二南里人 .

Some have argued from this that Lo (to whom the novel *Hsi-yang chi* is attributed on the strength of the same pen-name) was himself the author of the play,[120] but no preface or other sign of authorship appears in the modern reprint of the surviving copy in the Peking Library,[121] and it is impossible to judge how reliable the ascription is. In his preface of 1593 for the *Tseng-pu sou-shen chi* Lo represented himself as a satisfied customer obliging the publishers with an enthusiastic reaction, and this they were no doubt glad to print. The same could easily have happened again with the firm's *Hsiang-shan chi* in 1598.

We are in any case not concerned here with the literary standing of the play, which the ruthless critic Ch'i Piao-chia (1602–1645) dismissed as unworthy of any attention.[122] It is most certainly not an attempt to recast the Hsiang-shan story in an elegant literary form. For all its superficial editorial uniformity with other literary dramas of the late Ming, the play is clearly designed primarily for the stage, and in its latter scenes reflects specialised conventions of performance. The story as such suffers few changes of narrative importance,[123] but receives a different pattern of emphasis in presentation for the stage.

Discussions of the evolution of *ch'uan-ch'i* drama have taken the formal division and listing of named scenes (出) as one criterion for distinguishing early works from late. These characteristics are lacking in the earliest preserved texts but standard in the large published literature from the late Ming.[124] The *Hsiang-shan chi* is certainly so divided and is provided with a list of scenes at the beginning, together with a series of half-page illustrations — one for every couple of scenes.[125] But the titles listed at the opening are often at odds with the actual content of the numbered scenes in the text,[126] and the corresponding illustrations appear out of strict order and inserted at inappropriate points. Sawada Mizuho has also found the musical unity of the work forcibly broken up by the division into scenes.[127] All this suggests a brisk editorial attempt to bring an existing text into line with current publishing conventions — perhaps adapting a text from an earlier period.[128]

The play's theatricality requires little demonstration. It is evident enough from the frequent stage-directions calling on supporting players to come and dance or posture on the stage — whether demons and spirits performing tasks for Miao-shan (1.12b, 19b; 2.2ab) or summoning her to Hell (2.12a), or spirits of the wind and rain staging a storm (2.8a).[129] The play is full of such conventional stage business, but it takes on a more specialised and interesting character in the scenes which follow Miao-shan's death and delivery to Hell (sc. 21—25). These scenes perform three distinct functions: they carry the action of the story through necessary stages towards its later resolution (Miao-shan leaves the execution-ground on tiger-back; goes through Hell; meets Yama,[130] who explains her spiritual destiny; delivers the monks and nuns precipitated into Hell by their untimely death at her father's hands; is led off towards Hsiang-shan by a T'u-ti spirit); they briefly but importantly reaffirm Miao-shan's unchanging filial loyalty to her parents, a loyalty which she expresses and exercises in this context by urging her father's clerical victims to bear no resentment, and by transporting them to paradise (sc. 22); above all, they give a specific ritual character to all these actions.

This last function is important and distinctive enough to review in detail. In sc. 21 Miao-shan receives from the hands of Yama a 'skirt with yellow strings' 黃系裙, each of which has the power to deliver ten souls from the Citadel of the Unjustly Dead (Wang-ssu ch'eng), where the monks and nuns are held. The Golden Boy and Jade Girl then lead her on to meet these aggrieved souls. In sc. 22 she addresses them, pronouncing the words: 'I now deliver you to ascend the blue heaven', and then a stage direction causes the attendant demons to escort the souls out of the walled prison known as Kuei-men-kuan. Returning now to her own body, Miao-shan sets out in sc. 23 for her final destination. But the scene which follows (sc. 24) opens with a stage direction prescribing the performance of 'fifty-three salutations'[131] and followed by a brief and cryptic sung passage. The actions that must go with this are described in the scene's closing lines as 'paying homage to the Three Treasures' 朝三寶, and the effect is to establish Miao-shan with the full authority and power of Kuan-yin. She announces her new role as she stands in heavenly splendour at the beginning of sc. 25:

> Yesterday I completed my homage to the Buddhas. I now have the precious *Sūtra of the Lotus of the Wonderful Law* for the universal deliverance of the men of this world. I must read it out. (2.15b)

The scene is then bulked out with the complete text of the 'P'u-men p'in' section of the *sūtra* (2.15b—22b), at the end of which Kuan-yin looks down to the world below, sees her father sick and hastens to heal him.

With its long recitation this final intervening scene is, as Sawada Mizuho points out, both disproportionately long beside the other scenes in the play and most bizarre in making Kuan-yin herself recite the scripture whose very subject is Kuan-yin.[132] Its dramatic function seems even more obscure when we find the text accompanied by an illustration headed 'Recitation of *sūtras* for Universal Salvation' (宣經普度) and showing tonsured priests grouped around an altar with candles and censer. There is no indication in the text of the manner in which the *sūtra* is meant to be recited, nor indeed any specification of who should do it — apart from Miao-shan's own introductory words above. It is not clear whether the illustrator really envisaged a group of priests appearing on the stage to perform a purely liturgical rendering of the *sūtra*, or whether he was merely allowing the editorial title (attached to sc. 26 in the list of contents) to suggest to him its own style of representation.[133] But this open question brings to a head the ambiguity running right through the scenes we have just described. They present within a framework of *dramatic* action (the progress of Miao-shan's soul in the other-world) a series of *ritual* actions designed to assist the souls of the dead through their difficult passage to the after-life. The ambiguity is latent and unobtrusive in the early scenes (sc. 21—23), where we meet figures and tableaux from an other-world belonging equally to mythology, ritual and iconography. But in sc. 24 we witness an action which already seems to have more ritual than dramatic value, and in sc. 25 we are finally faced with a straightforward ritual episode standing clean outside the original action of the play, to the point that even the sixteenth-century illustrator presents it in purely ritual terms.

We shall argue in due course that this phenomenon, curtly dismissed by Sawada as a vulgar concession to a pietistic mass audience, has important implications for the interpretation of the story as a whole. Indeed the severe conclusions of Ch'i Piao-chia and Sawada — finding the play too vulgar in composition and appeal to carry conviction as the work of a literary author — prompt us to take a different approach. We can the more confidently see it as representing a popular tradition, perhaps more deeply rooted in time than its published date suggests, answering to other similar traditions elsewhere in China. Certainly, even in recent times, the story of Miao-shan could still be found enacted in a local ritual context.[134] The Fu-ch'un t'ang edition, unique as it appears to be within the remaining corpus of early 'Miao-shan' literature, may thus take us close to those elusive unwritten traditions living side by side with the more accessible and self-perpetuating narrative versions. Innocent of any sophisticated literary reworking, it offers a clearer idea of how the story of Miao-shan was used, what force it carried, in a popular medium that owed none of its conventions to the narrative tradition.

4. *The Spanish evidence*

THE reports of Martín de Rada and Miguel de Loarca have already served as an introduction to our study. They brought the Miao-shan story to Europe and this in itself was worthy of note. But they have for us the further value and interest of first-hand observations from precisely the period we have studied in this chapter. The Rada party visited various towns in Fukien during the summer of 1575, and one of their reports mentions Chien-ning fu as a centre of the printing and book trade.[135] They were thus moving in the very area and at the very time of the Chien-yang publishers' best documented activity, one product of which (in due course) was the novel *Nan-hai Kuan-yin ch'üan-chuan*.

Loarca's account of the story is explicit enough to stand comparison with the contemporary Chinese versions. But this comparison yields a tantalising mixture of striking similarities and quite unexpected deviations. The implications are not easy to assess. Before we can begin to think of identifying Loarca's Chinese source we have to allow for the errors of Spanish copyists, the uncertain conditions in which the original account was set down, the usual difficulties of finding things out through interpreters and informants. Several features of the story, particularly the proper names, are vulnerable to all these hazards. Others are liable to be interpreted and presented in the idiom and language of Western Catholicism, since it is clear from their comments that both Rada and Loarca tried to reconcile the story, which they apparently accepted as fact, with their own understanding of religious truth.

When all such obscuring factors are allowed for, Loarca still leaves us with interesting problems. His 'nunnery' episode is a detailed reflection of just such a version as we read in the *Hsiang-shan pao-chüan* or *Nan-hai Kuan-yin ch'üan-chuan*,[136] yet he says nothing of the visit to Hell which is integral to these and to every other version we know to have been current at the time. And his conclusion offers us something we find in no Chinese version — the almost playful gesture by which the girl puts a 'saint's image' on her head to be a fitting object for her father's embarrassing worship. Even if we care to attribute the minor variants in the 'nunnery' episode and the absence of the visit to Hell to Loarca's own unwitting, or deliberate, tinkering with the story, we can scarcely do the same with his conclusion. The gesture with the saint's image is too remarkable and important to be a casual addition, too unexpected to be developed from the story as it stands, too clearly worked out to be the result of misunderstanding. We must find some other way to explain it.

A likely answer seems to come when we read further in the travel accounts of the sixteenth-century missionaries. The Portuguese Dominican friar Gaspar da Cruz (d. 1570) visited Canton in the winter of 1556 and there saw a rather different form of the Kuan-yin cult. Like all interested travellers, he asked questions:

> In the city of Cantão ... I saw an oratory high from the ground very well made, with certain gilt steps before it, made of carved work, in which was a woman very well made with a child about her neck, and it had a lamp burning before it. I suspecting that to be some show of Christianity, asked of some laymen whom I found there, and of some of the idol's priests who were there, what that woman signified, and none could tell it me, nor give me any reason for it ... [137]

If Rada and his party saw some other form of Kuan-yin image and reacted in a similar way, they were evidently more successful. I have indeed myself, after expressing interest in the Kuan-yin altar of a temple in Hong Kong, been spontaneously treated to the Miao-shan story (in a confused and much simplified form) by a group of Taoist priests.[138] If something like this happened to the Rada party, we have a convincing way to explain the problem described above. An informant confronted with an image in a temple would naturally strive to account for its form at the same time as he told what he knew about the subject's mythology. In the present case he may have been faced with a Tantric-based form of Kuan-yin in which the figure of Amitābha was held above the head — a well-attested characteristic of 'Ta-pei' figures.[139] Another very different possibility is the grotesque and often monstrous paper figure known (with variants) as Ta-shih kung 大士公, representing a threatening manifestation of Kuan-yin, which sometimes bears a small image of the bodhisattva on the head-dress — the figure may still be seen among the Cantonese, Teochiu and Hokkien communities of South-East Asia, at the rituals of the Yü-lan season and other public and private ritual occasions.[140]

In such circumstances an informant's account of the well-known Miao-shan story would have to find a place for one of these forms at its climax, and he might well choose to simplify the story's shape and make free with its detail. Perhaps, indeed, Rada's informant knew the story in a form not quite like that preserved in our texts, although in other respects the echoes between his and other accounts are clear. But in any case the force of this explanation is to see in Loarca's version the reflection of a spontaneous personal retelling of the story in a certain situation to a certain audience. If this is close to the truth, then Loarca has given us a chance we rarely enjoy in our study of Chinese mythology — to penetrate beyond the texts to the environment in which they first appeared, and there glimpse the same stories passing between individuals by word of mouth.

5. *Reinterpretations*
WE set out to follow Miao-shan and her story from their point of departure to their widest distribution, and we have now seen them, near the close of the Ming dynasty, presented in versions which indeed secured a wide and lasting circulation. We have in passing also observed the story at large in other forms. In all this our constant concern has been to discover the *collective* impact of wide circulation on a story with specific local origins. We have chosen not to pursue individual and local variants for their own sake: they properly belong in locally based studies, which assemble specialised material gathered in the field and develop interpretations in the light of all relevant local particulars.

As a result of the broader approach adopted here it is almost time to turn from exposition of sources to a closer analysis of the story itself. For the many available treatments of the story from more recent times nearly all have a local or otherwise individual interest: few claim the kind of circulation which was long since achieved and maintained by the *Hsiang-shan pao-chüan*. But there is one exception, and we shall consider it both because it meets that basic test of circulation, and because it represents a style of treatment we do not find in the earlier sources. This is what we shall term 'reinterpretation': a conscious effort by an individual author to refashion the story in a form which answers to his own requirements or preoccupations.

A good early example (which will not be examined in detail here) is the play *Hai-ch'ao yin* 海潮音 by Chang Ta-fu, a seventeenth-century dramatist of Buddhist sympathies.[141] Chang evidently found the original story inadequately motivated. He added a new dimension to it by supplying a 'good angel' and 'evil angel' to guide the action, which thus became a symbolic struggle between true and false doctrines. His villain was a demon in Taoist guise, perverting the king's judgement into committing acts of barbarity; his celestial protagonist was an arhat, Shan-ssu Lo-han, responsible for guiding Miao-shan towards her due role as saviour of all living things. Many of the larger themes and minor features brought in by Chang Ta-fu can be traced to literary influences from the sixteenth and early seventeenth centuries. The play thus bears a 'period' stamp, and since there is little evidence that it was at all popular or well known it remains interesting to us only as a specimen of work by a certain author of a certain period.

These limitations do not, however, apply to a seventeenth-century reinterpretation in the *pao-chüan* form. The *Kuan-yin chi-tu pen-yüan chen-ching* 觀音濟度本願真經 has enjoyed a considerable circulation. Nineteenth-century copies survive in major *pao-chüan* collections and certain major libraries,[142] and the work is still in print in Taiwan.[143] The contents have been summarised in Dutch by Henri Borel.[144]

In form it follows familiar conventions. It is divided into two *chüan* and into twelve chapter-like headed divisions, each introduced and sometimes closed by the phrases usual in prose fiction. But its text is written in the *chantefable* style common to most *pao-chüan*, using loosely rhymed seven-syllable and ten-syllable (3—3—4) verse to expand or to further the basic prose narrative.

The evidence for authorship is bizarre, but does admit plausible conclusions. An impeccably Chinese preface is ascribed to Kuan-yin in person, who claims to have written the work as an accessible guide to salvation, and to have lodged it in a stone chamber in the holy cave Ch'ao-yüan tung on P'u-t'o shan. It bears a cyclical date which in one version is tied to the Ming Yung-lo reign, thus fixing the year at 1416.[145] This does little to help us. Another preface, signed 'Kuang-yeh shan-jen' 廣野山人, bears a precise date — January 1667 — and tells how the author, converted to the *Hsien-t'ien ta-tao* religion by a teacher with the syncretic title P'u-ting hsien-shih, once made a pilgrimage to P'u-t'o shan, was narrowly saved from shipwreck, and in the cave Ch'ao-yüan tung was given the text of Kuan-yin's own story. Finding it full of profound wisdom but written in a difficult Indian script, he 'transcribed' it (譯 寫 書 正) into an intelligible form and published it, so that its guidance in religious truth would be available to all.

This pious fiction of a dated autobiography by Kuan-yin need not detain us. The very improbability of finding and successfully transcribing a Chinese text (with preface) written in an Indian script is in itself enough to point plausibly to the preface-writer Kuang-yeh shan-jen as author of the whole fiction and hence the likeliest author of the *pao-chüan* itself. The evidence of the work as such is certainly consistent with this view. For while the framework of events in the story remains basically traditional, its system of incidental proper names betrays an affinity with the novel *Nan-hai Kuan-yin ch'üan-chuan*, which accords well with the mid-seventeenth-century dating.[146] Far more important, however, is the presentation of the story and the material added to it: in this respect the work is nothing less than a thoroughgoing reinterpretation in terms of the religion professed in his preface by Kuang-yeh shan-jen.

Hsien-t'ien ta-tao, the 'Great Way of Former Heaven', is a religious system known to us both from the evidence of traditional texts and from field study of the religion as practised in South China and South-East Asia. Its main features are: a millennial eschatology, which sees a sequence of three major cosmic cycles, each ending with a catastrophe; a cosmology and mythology formed from a synthesis of the Three Religions; worship of the primal void in the person of a female deity known as Mother; esoteric teaching leading suitable individuals towards an understanding of ultimate truth; self-cultivation, usually requiring sexual and dietary abstinence.[147]

Our present work is saturated with these teachings. They are voiced by the divine characters in the story as they debate and comment upon each stage of the action, and more directly by the narrator. Kuang-yeh shan-jen in his preface describes the work as a teaching text, and it is clearly designed to fulfil that function. A good example of how this is done comes up early in the story, at a point where Miao-shan has been isolated in the palace garden, bent on meditation and abstinence. The news is brought to the Buddha, who orders the ārya Bodhidharma to go to her and 'demonstrate the Great Way of Former Heaven'. Bodhidharma first tests her determination, then floods her with

The sixteenth and seventeenth centuries 71

technical questions...

'Where will you set about looking for the Root of your Nature?
Where is your Mother's place?
Who is your Original (本來人)?
Where does one dwell in the Perfect Good?
May I hear if you know how to dwell in Quietude?
How does one "exhaust one's nature and return to the beginning" (厥性復初)?
How are Pure and Impure (清濁) to be distinguished?
If you do not understand these principles in your cultivation
Mere vague vegetarianism is wasted effort —
You will only be free from your debt to the six animals,
But you cannot escape rebirth in the Red Dust.
From their parents people get an impure *yin* body;
If you do not know how to eliminate the *yin*, how will the *yang* come forth?'

The princess, we read, then lowers her head and thinks: 'Perhaps the Buddha is delivering me.' She at once bows to the powers of Heaven and Hell, Buddhist and Taoist, solemnly vowing to seek the Way of Former Heaven.[148]

Thus a single passage, in deliberately bewildering esoteric language, affirms by name the religion of Kuang-yeh shan-jen, alludes to Mother,[149] borrows freely from Buddhist and Taoist teachings and invokes deities without discrimination. The same approach is pursued and developed consistently throughout the work.

This much is common property of the whole 'Great Way' system. But the author also has more particular concerns. The opening lines of his text seem to address a female audience: Kuan-yin surveys the society of China and finds it appallingly steeped in sin, but whereas the men have a redeeming capacity to grasp the Truth, the women seem hopelessly benighted...

'I had best go to the world below, take on a woman's body and undo the calamity of the five stages of impurity[150] as an example to future generations, so that women will know their sins and reform. They will avoid the suffering of rebirth, escape the punishments of Hell, the retribution of the Bloody River, and set out together on the road to enlightenment, enjoy the beautiful scenes of paradise. Only this will fulfil my vow.'[151]

The special message to women is more fully spelled out later in the story, when Miao-shan explains to her parents her objections to accepting a conventional woman's destiny: even if she remains a model of womanly virtue, the bearing of children and the taking of life will leave her tainted with blood which offends the ancestral shrine, the gods of the hearth and the waters, the heaven, sun, moon and stars; Yama will exact justice for it in Hell; Miao-shan's religious cultivation is necessary to redeem her from this fate.[152] Such a deliberate articulation of women's ritual needs brings out an appeal to women which was always latent in the traditional story of Miao-shan. It also associates the present work with a modest but enduring corpus of *pao-chüan* exploring the same theme, and it remains consistent with the values of the *Hsien-t'ien ta-tao* religion, whose sects are noted for their care and protection of women's interests.[153] Here again there is reason to believe that the seventeenth-century author was reacting to a popular literary climate well developed in his own time. It seems likely that the *Kuan-yin chi-tu pen-yüan chen-ching* owes much of its circulation and survival to an untiring female public whose social plight and characteristic piety have remained unchanged until modern times. Below, in discussing the interpretation of the legend, we shall pay closer attention to this significant social and literary context.

The author had one even more specialised preoccupation, which led him to include a remarkable episode in the story of Miao-shan's adventures at the nunnery Po-ch'üeh ssu. Having passed through the formalities of entry to a Buddhist establishment, Miao-shan goes on to explore the buildings and finds a hall dedicated to the Taoist Triad — San-ch'ing tien 三清殿. Half concealed at the rear is a chamber marked 'Place of Perfect Good' 至善之地 (recalling an earlier esoteric reference quoted above). It is the Taoist chamber of Huang chang-lao 黃長老, who keeps it in perpetual darkness. He welcomes her cheerfully inside, and they at once establish a close rapport. The verse passage which describes the mysteries exchanged between them is couched in the densely metaphorical language of Taoist *nei-tan* writings. This retreat into metaphor while Miao-shan stays alone with a Taoist master in a darkened chamber leaves the reader (perhaps by design) with a sense of uncertainty. The ambiguity is exploited before long in the story: a children's song circulates among the people alleging, in thinly disguised and mocking terms, that the king's daughter is cohabiting with a Taoist in the San-ch'ing tien. The king's rage at this suggestion prompts him to have the Po-ch'üeh ssu burned down.[154]

The 'San-ch'ing tien' episode is the author's most radical addition to the traditional Miao-shan story. But the symbolism and implied doctrine of *nei-tan* Taoism continue to echo through the text as a whole. They represent perhaps the most personal element in a rich, allusive fabric of interpretation, and add to the complexity and interest of the work.

Waley found the *Kuan-yin chi-tu pen-yüan chen-ching* a 'long and rather tedious' retelling of the Miao-shan legend,[155] and no doubt, if judged solely on aesthetic merits, it would remain unprinted and unread. Yet it survives to claim a value of another kind: a document which we can relate to fictional sources, to sectarian doctrine, and to a specific readership. It therefore adds usefully to our knowledge of the 'uncertain boundaries between religion, literature and entertainment' which we have recognised as the home territory of the Miao-shan legend.

5 Anatomy of the story

LOOKING BACK through this written tradition we find the Miao-shan story gaining and losing episodes and details as it passes through different circumstances. At several points we have tried to explain additions and changes in relation to their context, and we shall attempt before long to form a broad impression of the story's course of development. The whole process begins, however, with a given, ready-made version of the story at a fixed point in time — January 1100. The evidence offers nothing earlier. If we wish, then, to learn something of the composition of that first, basic document we must turn to internal evidence. Certainly, the history of the two monasteries at the legend's birthplace uncovers a strong local element in the early story: the name Hsiang-shan, the Po-ch'üeh ssu, the *stūpa* and its related manifestation of the Thousand-armed and Thousand-eyed Bodhisattva — all these are features the story seems to owe to its first known environment. But having allowed for them, we are still left with a coherent story possessing its own marked characteristics. Its learned critics, from Chu Pien in the twelfth century to Tsukamoto and Waley in the twentieth have been uneasily aware that, while it bears all the marks of a Buddhist derivation, it lacks any discoverable precedent in Buddhist literature. So (unless we are content to accept Tao-hsüan's angelic visitation) there is still no straightforward answer to the natural question — what was the source of the text shown to Chiang Chih-ch'i? The answer can only be sought indirectly. In what follows, we shall begin by annotating a number of details in the story which have some recognisable

— usually Buddhist — antecedents, and then consider what remains.

1. *Annotations*
(a) The prescriptions of the Hsiang-shan hermit.

In the Tsu-hsiu/Chüeh-lien version Miao-shan's father suffers a disease with a Sanskrit name, *kāmalā*, usually identified with jaundice;[156] he is directed to seek a 'divine remedy' (神方) from an immortal (仙人) on Hsiang-shan, to make 'medicine' (藥) from it, and thus recover his health.[157]

All this terminology is echoed in the title of a book recorded in an early bibliography. The *Hsiang-shan hsien-jen yao-fang* 香山仙人藥方, in ten *chüan*, appears as an entry in the medical section of the famous bibliographical chapters of the *Sui-shu*.[158] The text is not preserved. For our information on it we depend on clues gathered from the title and the context of its citation. The name 'Hsiang-shan' implies a Buddhist reference, and the term *hsien-jen* has a Buddhist as well as a Taoist usage (it renders the Sanskrit *ṛṣi*, and its range of meanings can include 'ascetic', 'hermit'). More particularly, the bibliographical entry is grouped with medical titles associated explicitly with the Western Regions and with Brahminical traditions. The '*ṛṣi*' element appears several times in the list. The signs thus seem clear that this title represents a lost medical text of Indian origin, although no Sanskrit original has been identified. It was known in the seventh century, but we cannot be sure that it survived into the twelfth. Conceivably the text, or some related tradition, was known to the author of the Miao-shan story, who, prompted by the 'Hsiang-shan' reference, derived from it his Sanskrit illness and *ṛṣi* healer. The speculation is a bold one, but it does offer a possible insight into the arresting medical details of the story.

(b) The bodhisattva's arms and eyes.

In Buddhist Jātaka literature the bodhisattva's liberality to the point of self-mutilation is a standard theme. Gifts of flesh, eyes, head and body are well attested in Chinese Buddhist sources.[159] The filial sacrifice of flesh to succour ailing parents can also be found in Buddhist parable literature,[160] and becomes a stereotyped gesture in later Chinese *exempla* of filial piety.[161] But in our story the specific surrendering of arms and eyes is linked to an iconographical form — Ta-pei, with a thousand arms and eyes — through an act of miraculous restoration and revelation:

> The holy one [Miao-shan] said: 'I suffer no pain. Having yielded up my mortal eyes I shall receive diamond eyes; having given up my human arms I shall receive gold-coloured arms. If my vow is true these results will certainly follow.'[162] The queen was about to lick the eyes with her tongue, but before she could do so auspicious clouds enclosed all around, divine musicians began to play, the earth shook, flowers rained down. And then the holy manifestation of the Thousand Arms and Thousand Eyes was revealed hovering majestically in the air.[163]

It is a scene which vividly recalls another, recounted in chapter 23 of the *Lotus sūtra* — the chapter whose subject is the Bodhisattva Yao-wang ('Medicine-King'). This bodhisattva, at the time under the name Hsi-chien, burns off his arms in homage before *stūpas* containing relics of the Buddha. Then, amid the consternation of all assembled, he performs an Act of Truth:

> 'Having given up both my arms, I shall (yet) assuredly obtain a buddha's golden body. If this (assurance) be true and not false, let both my arms be restored as they were before.' As soon as he had made this vow (his arms) were of themselves restored, (all) brought to pass through the excellence of this bodhisattva's felicitous virtue and wisdom. At that moment the three-thousand-great-thousandfold world was shaken in the six ways, the sky rained various flowers, and gods and men all attained that which they had never before experienced.[164]

The chapter goes on to describe how the bodhisattva's deed and its sacred record can heal sickness and lead to favourable rebirths.

It is more than a picturesque scene. There is a complex of echoes. In both texts the sacrificed arms are restored in a magnificent celestial triumph and the bodhisattva is simultaneously revealed as healer and saviour; the 'golden body' of the 'Medicine-King's' vow is echoed by the 'diamond eyes' and 'golden-coloured arms' of Miao-shan's vow.[165] The most significant circumstance, moreover, is that this parallel comes from

Anatomy of the story

the latter chapters of the *Lotus sūtra*, one of which — chapter 25, the *P'u-men p'in* — is the cardinal Kuan-yin scripture, perhaps more familiar to the Chinese world than any other sacred text. It turns out, indeed, that these late chapters of the *Lotus* provide material for much of the Miao-shan story's substance and incidental detail.

(c) King Miao-chuang-yen.[166]

His name, in Sanskrit Śubhavyūha, heads chapter 27 of the *Lotus sūtra*, and the chapter tells his story. His wife's name faintly recalls that of Miao-shan's mother,[167] but his story recalls hers more strongly. He is one who 'believes in the heretics and is deeply attached to the Brahman Law', while his two sons have mastered the ways of the bodhisattvas. They long to enlighten him, and at their mother's suggestion perform a series of supernatural feats to convince him of their spiritual attainments. He is duly impressed and convinced. Urged on by his sons, he leads his ministers and retinue in a great procession to visit the Buddha, who preaches to him and accepts him into the order, announcing great future achievements. The king then makes over his kingdom to his younger brother, and together with his queen, sons and retinue he forsakes his home to accept the rule of the Buddha. In the end, after ecstatic contemplation of the Buddha and due acknowledgement that he owes this to his sons, the king becomes a bodhisattva, and with him the members of his family. One of his sons indeed becomes that very Bodhisattva Yao-wang ('Medicine-King') who sacrificed and recovered his arms in chapter 23.

The parallels between *Lotus sūtra* and Hsiang-shan legend are nowhere closer than here, where they touch the story's essential situation: a 'heretical' king led towards the true doctrine by filial offspring, renouncing his secular dominion and committing himself with family and followers to the Buddha's rule, after a sumptuous royal progress to the seat of the holy one. In short, the 'Śubhavyūha' chapter gives the Hsiang-shan legend its religious theme, some of its personalities, and the form of its climax and conclusion. And for the closing gestures of cremation, preservation of relics and building of a *stūpa*, the author could find a model once more in chapter 23 of the *Lotus*, where the *parinirvāṇa* of a buddha is followed by the gathering of his relics into urns and the erection of *stūpas* (those same *stūpas* before which the future Bodhisattva Yao-wang

sacrifices his arms).[168]
(d) Miao-yen, Miao-yin and Miao-shan.

Tsu-hsiu and Chüeh-lien give the three sisters exactly the same set of names. Of the three, Miao-yin and Miao-shan remain standard in virtually every later version of the story. Miao-yen appears only this once.

They come from different backgrounds. Miao-yin is the name of an important bodhisattva, Gadgadasvara, familiar to most Chinese as the subject of chapter 24 in the *Lotus sūtra*. Like Avalokiteśvara he is a universal saviour, and in the long list of forms adopted by him to work salvation among all categories of the living, the line which perhaps most struck the author of the Hsiang-shan legend was: 'Even in the inner courts of a king, transforming himself into a woman, he preaches this Sutra'.[169] The canonical Miao-yen performs a similar function: he is the hero of a little story in which, as an eight-year-old novice, he enters the palace of King Aśoka, firmly resists the queen's maternal embrace, and preaches the Law to her and the five hundred ladies-in-waiting.[170]

Yet in the Hsiang-shan legend the sister who sets herself to preach in the palace is the third, with a different but cognate name — Miao-shan. It appears as a name or epiphet in a variety of Buddhist contexts, sometimes as the name of a bodhisattva.[171] More particularly, again in the *Sui-shu*, there is a passage which applies the hyperbolic description '*Miao-shan p'u-sa*' 妙善菩薩 to a recently deceased empress.[172] It is surely not fair to claim here a connection with the later female Kuan-yin and the Hsiang-shan legend[173] — certainly no such connection is expressed — but the phrase does suggest that this name was linked in Chinese usage with the notion of a bodhisattva manifest in womanly form.

The names and themes discussed in these annotations point clearly to the *Lotus sūtra* (in particular the group of so-called 'additional chapters',[174] with their brilliant visions of spiritual triumph and message of universal salvation) as the strongest single influence in the Hsiang-shan legend's composition. A smaller number of exotic elements in the story can be associated with other Buddhist or Indian sources. If, hypothetically, we regard all this as part of the 'Hsiang-shan' author's raw material, we can infer a 'melting-pot' process of composition, in which themes and names from the *Lotus* and cer-

Anatomy of the story

tain other traditions come together with the firm data of a local situation to form a new synthetic story. In this new creation the name and spiritual career of King Śubhavyūha remain essentially intact, and the other names and themes are grouped around him, surrendering some of their original distinctive identity. The work has been neatly done. By borrowing Miao-yin from the *Lotus*, Miao-yen and Miao-shan from elsewhere, the author has contrived a 'Chinese' family group which shares (though with spurious philology) a family name 'Miao'. By causing the bodhisattva to sacrifice arms *and* eyes, he makes possible her final transfiguration in the form of the Ta-pei image for which Hsiang-shan was known.

2. *King Lear*

THE story itself remains unaccounted for. At the centre of this grandiose religious fable, peopled by extravagantly named characters from the scriptures and climaxed by a scene of apocalyptic triumph, is a tale about a father displeased with his youngest daughter because of her determined refusal to marry, but who, when he has tried to destroy her and thinks himself rid of her, relies on her heroic assistance to relieve his suffering, and finally admits she is in the right. Since this is what remains when all other identifiable circumstance is stripped away, we shall call it the 'kernel story'. It is a story we instinctively recognise. For those brought up with European literature it at once recalls *King Lear* — also a work whose ancestry traces back through a complicated system of antecedents to a documentary source of the twelfth century. Beyond that point, however, scholarship is obliged to seek an ultimate source in unwritten folk tradition.[175] We now find ourselves in the same position.

The analysis of folktales is a study whose aims, assumptions and techniques differ from those of the present work, and no attempt will be made here to pursue it. But we are bound to acknowledge an extensive literature of collected tales which, more or less closely, resemble Miao-shan's kernel story. Two groupings, from India and China, will serve as our sample.[176] Each represents, in the words of Stith Thompson, 'a practical listing of tales for a certain area, so that collectors and scholars can have a common base of reference.'[177] Thus, although the groups of tales are organised in a scheme of numbered 'types', it does not follow, and is not accepted here, that the types are clearly defined theoretical categories. The tales themselves mostly reach us at some removes from the local vernacular milieux from which they claim to come. Their incidence and form are at the discretion of collectors and editors. As data they can neither be verified nor otherwise controlled. We shall therefore not venture any but the most generalised remarks about them.

The common features of the selected Indian tales are summarised under the title 'The princess who was responsible for her own fortune' —

> I. *Judgement.* When a king asks his daughters who is responsible for their good fortune, or the like, the oldest daughters answer that he is, but the youngest, who says that she alone is, is (a) married to a poor man, cripple, or the like and forced to live with him in humble circumstances or (b) driven forth. (c) The story concerns a king and his sons.
> II. *Daughter's Success.* (a) Through her wit or her skill she makes the poor man rich and eventually makes him a king or cures him of his disease. (b) The husband magically changes into a handsome prince or (c) She becomes wealthy and later marries a prince.
> III. *Reconciliation.* (a) The father visits the new king, recognises his daughter, and is forced to admit she is responsible for her own fortune. (b) The father has, in the meantime, lost his kingdom and wanders to the palace of his daughter. He is forced to admit that she is responsible for her own fortune.[178]

The Eberhard synopsis of the Chinese tales is consistent with this, and although some elements are differently phrased ('rich man' instead of 'king'; 'fate' instead of individual responsibility), there is give and take between the actual tales of the two groups even on these points. For practical purposes, the two groups share as much coherence as either of them possesses.

The tales cover a wide range of circumstances and assume a more or less complicated form, sometimes accommodating or merging into other stories. It is therefore all the more striking that, in the midst of this indiscriminate and colourful variety, the simple 'kernel story' of Miao-shan stands out strongly for one unique feature. Alone in some fifty stories it rests its motivation upon a daughter's specific commitment to a religious discipline and consequent refusal to marry. The fact that she stands by this principle rather than any other naturally frustrates the 'successful marriage' at the heart of most of the other tales, but it also obliges the story to find its resolution quite outside the framework of a secular society. It is fundamental to this and all the tales of our sample that the rebellious daughter should be acknowledged right in the end, and the kernel story of Miao-shan duly requires her father to submit to the religion whose discipline outrages his secular principles. It is precisely the conflict which we found so elaborately debated in the *Hsiang-shan pao-chüan*: a formal confrontation between the conventional social demands of Chinese life and the contrary demands of a code of religious abstinence. For many in the traditional Chinese world it was a serious issue, and its successful resolution certainly contributed to Miao-shan's survival and popularity in certain sections of Chinese society.

The value of our sample of folktales lies here. Against this untidy but loosely homogeneous background we see how firmly even the 'kernel story' of Miao-shan fixed its attention on the conflict between secular and monastic ideals.

3. *Development before and after 1100*

THE actual process of composition behind the text copied by Huai-chou and shown to Chiang Chih-ch'i can only be guessed at. But the evidence discussed here does suggest a number of stages with their own logical and perfectly credible sequence. Even though we cannot know whether this corresponds to an actual sequence in time, it provides a convenient form in which to summarise our findings.

The sequence begins with a tale in popular circulation, dealing in some form with the common theme of an independent-minded youngest daughter cast out by her father, establishing herself successfully in a new life elsewhere, then rallying to her stricken father's aid and accepting his penitent surrender in a final reconciliation. The tale is then taken and refashioned in a committed, even polemical, religious form. It receives a cast of named scriptural characters, a body of specific incident, and a clearly defined location — elements drawn from various quarters (the *Lotus sūtra*, other Buddhist sources, local associations of the two Pao-feng monasteries) but so closely woven together that we cannot easily separate out an order of priority. One further step brings us finally to Chiang Chih-ch'i's text: the 'frame' story presenting the whole as a divine revelation to Tao-hsüan and confirming the geographical position of the holy site.

Let us repeat that this is no more than a convenient form in which to set out the anatomy of the story we find at the head of our tradition. And it is well to remember that the tradition itself, although pursued above through a chronological series of texts, is not a precisely documented historical phenomenon. The texts have a life of their own, and whatever we gather about their traditional background is gathered indirectly. We shall therefore not attempt the impractical task of establishing a strict chronology of development, but continue to trace a pattern of *formal* development as we find it implied in the sources. This pattern may loosely fit the sequence of texts discussed above, but chronology is less important to it than internal criteria.

Three formal stages stand out. *First*, the story as we have it from the hand of Tsu-hsiu (1164) and of Chüeh-lien (1551), and which we presume to stand close to the work of Chiang Chih-ch'i. Within its grandiose Buddhist frame of reference the story remains simple in form, playing out a single, organic action. The king and his daughter are separated by their crucially different views on marriage; while she departs to pursue her spiritual career elsewhere, he incurs a heavy weight of *karma* by vindictively taking the lives of nuns; with her gift of arms and eyes, the daughter relieves the suffering brought upon him by his act and draws him to her in penitence; his submission to Buddhism secures his salvation and reveals the fruits of the Bodhisattva's work in the world of men. It is an uncomplicated action in which each element is causally related to the whole and necessary to its unbroken flow of motivation and development.

A *second stage* is reached when, in the 'circulating' versions of the story, Miao-shan submits to execution, descends to Hell and there delivers the damned from their sufferings. Her act of deliverance takes different forms, ranging from the specific redemption of those monks and nuns that her father has rushed to untimely death (*Hsiang-shan chi*) to the catholic recitation of *sūtras* for the benefit of all suffering sinners (Kuan Tao-sheng)

Several versions include both. With the episode go other conspicuous but at first sight random features: the tiger that appears on the execution-ground to bear off Miao-shan's body into the forest, and the peach which she is given on her return from the underworld as she sets out for Hsiang-shan. In themselves these elements can each be given a ritual gloss: the meritorious recitation of *sūtras* and the saving intervention of Kuan-yin in Hell (with its clear background of scriptural authority) play a familiar and essential part in Chinese ritual for the benefit of the dead;[179] the tiger and peach have an ancient and enduring protective function at points of ritual transition.[180] But the episode which brings such elements into the story of Miao-shan breaks open its simple, self-consistent framework and creates one more complex and problematical.

The story's first stage shaped itself around a single central climax: the sacrifice of the daughter's arms and eyes. But now the climax is pre-empted by the sacrifice of life itself. Although the original sacrifice remains necessary for a final resolution of the action, it pales beside the splendours of the new episode. The story's second stage thus places a strain on the sense of form to which the first so clearly appealed. The strain is felt even if the new episode enters into the story's domestic scheme as an action specifically designed to redeem the king's evil *karma*: for when, as in the play *Hsiang-shan chi*, Miao-shan delivers the monks and nuns whose resentful souls threaten her father, she strikes at the root of his karmic sufferings; her later sacrifice of arms and eyes adds little to this redemptive action, beyond giving the father mere physical relief and a reunion with his daughter. In many versions moreover, the episode in Hell makes larger claims still by affirming Kuan-yin's power of universal salvation. It steps beyond the bounds of the original action and becomes public, not private property. The story now presents a challenge to the interpreter. Either it is unintelligible — clumsily hacked open to allow a gratuitous excursion into standard piety — or it must be read in a way which makes sense of its new and confusing form. Our final chapter will return to this task.

The textual sources show a further, *third stage* of development, encompassing and expanding upon the other two. It is the stage in which the developed story gains many episodic appendages from different hands at different times. These episodes appear at certain 'open' points in the story, where its basic action has a moment of rest and can tolerate the insertion of new material: the very opening, where introductory accounts of the main characters' previous existence can be harmlessly supplied; the 'nunnery' scene, which can be enriched with as many adventures as the author desires; the royal journey to Hsiang-shan, a classic invitation to episodic treatment which can be further complicated by false starts and repetitions. The appendages proper to this third stage are alike incidental and transitory. They temporarily ornament or clutter the story, but do not distort its essential logic and shape. In this they are quite different from the visit to Hell of the second stage, which represents a permanent structural feature of the developed story. The third-stage episodes are superficial and nearly always unproblematical. They can be explained by reference to the context and formal requirements of the works in which they appear. Several of them have already been examined above, and we shall not discuss them further.

Beyond this point the story enters territory which our study has not attempted to explore. To define any subsequent stages of development it will be necessary to turn to those local traditions which by design we have left for future specialised research, and to examine how the multitude of local circumstances have reshaped the story to local needs. The formal framework of textual material outlined here will perhaps make the task easier to undertake.

6 Interpretations

1. *A charter for celibacy*

THE OLD LITURGICAL TEXT *Chin-kang k'o-i* puts it like this: 'Miao-shan refused to take a husband, and most certainly achieved buddhahood.'[181] Like the historical Buddha, she rejected the privileged secular life into which she had been born and rose to spiritual triumph. To those who read it in this light the story thus serves as a charter for dedicated celibacy, and we find in its most widely circulating versions — particularly the *Hsiang-shan pao-chüan* — a vigorous apologia for the life of religious renunciation. The successful impact of this appeal is reflected indirectly in the survival of the texts themselves, which depended on generations of pious donation and circulation. But its context and rationale must be sought and tested in traditional Chinese society as such (so far as modern conditions allow us to know it), and they are most clearly seen among women, for whom the choice between marriage and celibacy carried the most crucial implications for success and failure in secular or religious life.

In orthodox secular society a woman's unquestionable duty was to marry at her parents' behest and thereafter submit her will to husband, and in due course, son. Society could offer secular compensations and rewards for a position which seemed in many ways vulnerable and thankless,[182] but marriage and secular womanhood brought with them sufferings and ritual dangers of the kind we have seen Miao-shan describe to her parents in the *Kuan-yin chi-tu pen-yüan chen-ching*.[183] The taint of unclean blood which beset women in childbirth and in many other aspects of their working life put them at a great disadvantage in their pursuit of religious merit and their hopes of deliverance from human sufferings. Their troubles are summed up in this homely but eloquent passage:

> For ten months, while a girl is in her mother's womb, she turns her back to her mother, facing outward, staying aloof. If the mother moves about, the unborn child begins to stir. When the child is born everyone is disgusted. While the child is in the womb, the mother suffers as if in prison; once the child is out of the womb the mother meets only disgust. Everyone in the family, young and old, is displeased, objecting to us women for being born to our mothers. Our parents have no choice but to raise us, and when we grow up we are married to someone else ... When our husband's parents are angry we must hasten to please them with smiles. When our husband furiously curses us we must not answer back. If we slit or tear fine fabrics, it is a sinful crime, and it's a serious offence if we drop the basket in the water when washing rice. We taint heaven and earth when we give birth to children, and in washing filth from our bloodstained skirts we offend the river gods. If we put on make-up we attract attention and are punished for flouting the law as loose women. If our parents-in-law are kind, we may see our own families once or twice in a year. But if we don't meet with their approval we will never return to our homes again ... Once you are married to a husband you are under his control for your whole life: all your pleasures and miseries are at his discretion. When you are a man's wife you are bound to know the sufferings of childbirth, you cannot avoid the bloodstained water, and the sin of offending the sun, moon and stars.

The bleak sermon concludes:

> If you are a wise and clever woman, you will eat vegetarian food, recite the Buddha's name and start religious cultivation at once. How favoured and honoured you will be when you migrate from a woman's to a man's body! In your next existence you can once again follow the way to the Pure Land.[184]

Here are both diagnosis and remedy. Womanhood itself,

inevitably implying marriage, is seen as an evil to be escaped from. Those caught in that wretched and offensive state of life have only one thing to hope for — rebirth as a male, with the further hope of paradise in a later existence; and it must be earned through standard religious merit-building activities. But the logic of this embittered and desperate analysis can be taken a step further. A woman who avoids marriage also avoids the indignities and ritual dangers to which it exposes her. Her accumulation of religious merit will be correspondingly stronger and more effective. So it is that some women in traditional society took their resistance to marriage to the point of actual defiance. It could mean suicide.[185] But there was (apart from certain low-status occupations open to unattached women) the institutional refuge of the Buddhist or Taoist priesthood. In some parts of China there were also communities specially dedicated to the maintenance and welfare of women pursuing a life of religious celibacy and vegetarianism. They were frequently associated with the minority devotional religions mentioned above, and their activities can still be observed in parts of South-East Asia.[186]

The socially rebellious teaching of these minority religions served a wider audience than the determined but small group of women who actually withdrew from orthodox social life. It was vividly propagated through a specialised *pao-chüan* literature in which women of all ages and conditions vicariously found their problems confronted and miraculously resolved. These *pao-chüan* — among them the text just quoted — served that zealous but less radical piety which has so consistently been observed among the women of traditional Chinese society. It comes as no surprise that Dr. Topley found them regularly used as leisure reading material in the 'vegetarian communities' of single women.[187] But several scenes in the sixteenth-century *Chin P'ing Mei tz'u-hua* illustrate what must have been a common enough situation in *secular* life: groups of married women regularly engaging professional nuns to recite for them, *en famille*, the texts they found relevant to their spiritual needs.[188] The most extended of these scenes sets out at length the *Huang-shih nü chüan* 黃氏女卷, a good representative example of the 'problem-solving' *pao-chüan* that concern us here. In a characteristic *chantefable* style it tells of a pious and virtuous girl who early in life sees Kuan-yin in a vision; but she lives to be married and bear children to a butcher — that most polluting of occupations. She proposes that they devote themselves to religious cultivation, but her husband refuses and leaves her. Her lonely piety draws the attention of Yama, who summons her to the Underworld. Reluctantly accepting death and mourned by her children, she is shown through Hell, where she gives more evidence of her piety. She then achieves a male rebirth, grows up clever and successful, and becomes an official in her old home county. In this way the reborn mother can be united with her original family. The story ends with an apotheosis in which Huang-shih's original religious values are seen to triumph.[189]

A whole class of *pao-chüan* explores the fates of other such pious women at odds with their secular destiny. Typically, the women marry, if at all, with reluctance; they suffer grievously at the hands of their husband's family; some are reduced to death and, like Huang-shih, pass through Hell before returning to the world of the living; but finally these women triumph over their disadvantages by gaining a spiritual authority to which their persecutors bow.[190]

Without question Miao-shan claims a place, and a pre-eminent place, among the heroines of this specialised religious literature. Her challenge to the marriage institution is more radical and more successful than theirs: she resists even the proposal that she should take a husband. For her the stakes are higher than for them: she rejects not the mixed sufferings of common womanhood, but the privileged and protected life of a royal princess. But then her sufferings are still more grievous than theirs: she submits to the humiliation of public execution at the hands, not of a hostile alien family, but of her own kin. And finally her triumph is immeasurably greater than theirs: as the Bodhisattva Kuan-yin she ranks with the highest in the Chinese pantheon, a universal saviour of mankind. In theme, detail and form many of the 'companion' works described here could indeed be directly patterned upon the story of Miao-shan (though it should be noted that a very similar story existed, apparently quite independently, as the subject of a traditional 'harvest festival' ritual drama in Tibet).[191] But questions of priority and influence are here secondary to the function which the stories fulfilled. Miao-shan did in practice serve many as an outstanding example sanctioning the socially unorthodox life of

Interpretations

religious celibacy. Dr. Topley observes: 'We have had this story quoted to us several times by vegetarians as a justification for their own single state'.[192] The roots of such a view extend deep into the 'pre-history' of the legend, and we have seen it elaborately and polemically debated in the widely circulating *pao-chüan* versions. There can be no doubt that some good part of the Miao-shan story's importance in traditional China lay in its supremely triumphant solution to the problems of religious celibacy in a secular society where family life and family loyalty exerted absolute claims.

A reading which, like this, sets the story in a social context and relates it to particular social problems has the advantage of being easy to document and verify. But such a reading also narrows attention to one theme, one function, and blurs all other distinctions. It fits the story easily but loosely, taking no account of the 'anatomical' complexities discussed above. Chüeh-lien, for instance, was able to gloss the line 'Miao-shan refused to take a husband' both clearly and adequately without reference to the 'visit to Hell' of the story's second stage. And similarly, some of the companion *pao-chüan* on pious women deliver their wronged heroines without subjecting them to the outrage of violent death.[193] Yet it remains a fact that other *pao-chüan*, like the second-stage Miao-shan stories, do shape themselves around a central complex of untimely death, passage through Hell, and return to the living world.[194] Taken as a whole, the companion *pao-chüan* literature thus echoes that formal distinction between 'first' and 'second' stages which we drew above in our anatomy of the Miao-shan story. To read these stories as a 'charter for celibacy' leaves the distinction still unexplained, since all, with or without a 'death, Hell, rebirth' complex, admit that simple interpretation equally well. Yet the complex appears so often that, as a common formal feature, it requires its own explanation.[195] We shall eventually have to account for the formal difference between the 'first' and 'second' stages and show exactly what the recurrent 'death, Hell, rebirth' sequence contributes to the shape and meaning of the whole.

2. *A supreme act of filial piety*

EMBEDDED in the very earliest forms of the story is another vital and enduring theme, this time part of the main fabric of traditional Chinese life. In a special sense we have here a classic of filial piety.

Miao-shan gives up her arms and eyes as freely as the Bodhisattva in the Jātakas gave up his most treasured possessions. But with her the gesture is not an act of totally disinterested, random liberality, as the terms of Buddhist perfection clearly require, but a means of support and reconciliation in the supremely sensitive relationship between father and child. Moreover her father is the namesake of that king who, in the *Lotus sūtra*, was led to the Truth by his devoted sons. Her story, like his, dramatises a situation which we find discussed and explained more than once in early Buddhist writings, and which assumed great importance in the acceptance of Buddhism in Chinese life. In one early passage the Buddha proclaims:

> Parents do a great deal for their child. They feed him, raise him, devote constant care in bringing him up so that in all ways he comes to full growth. Even if a son spent a thousand years bearing his father on his right shoulder and his mother on the left, even if he let them relieve themselves over his back without bearing them any resentment, such a son would still not have done enough to repay his parents' love. But if his parents lacked faith and he brought them to faith, they would find some peace . . .

The passage goes on to list the other Buddhist perfections which a filial son should help his parents to acquire.[196] In the *Divyāvadāna*, an early collection of Buddhist legends, this same idea is explored by the Buddha's great disciple Maudgalyāyana, the Chinese Mu-lien. He recalls words of the Buddha:

> If a son who has received initiation and discipline establishes his faithless parents in the perfection of faith, if he gives the perfection of morality to parents whose morals are bad, that of liberality to avaricious parents, that of knowledge to ignorant parents — this son will have done good to his father and mother; he will have repaid them what he owed them.[197]

The lesson prompts Maudgalyāyana to serve his lost mother accordingly.

The Buddhist movement in China made vigorous use of this appeal to filial piety. Here was a way to compensate for that

Interpretations

aspect of Buddhist practice most at odds with Chinese ethical values — the separation from family life and retreat to the monastic community. Both Mu-lien and Śākyamuni himself came to be credited with filial motives in their renunciation of secular society and attainment of spiritual perfection,[198] and in Mu-lien, as is well known, we have the dominating figure of redemptive filial piety in Chinese popular mythology. Miao-shan too belongs in this company: renouncing secular life, she performed for her father the unique filial service of leading him to the true doctrine. When asked for her arms and eyes, she said (according to Tsu-hsiu):

> 'My father showed disrespect to the Three Treasures, he persecuted and suppressed the True Doctrine, he executed innocent nuns. This called for retribution.' Then she gladly cut out her eyes and severed her arms. Giving them to the envoy, she added instructions to exhort the king to turn towards the good, no longer to be deluded by false doctrines.

Against this background the scene of reunion takes on a richer significance:

> 'Does My Lady remember Miao-shan? Mindful of my father's love, I have repaid him with my arms and eyes.'

Her father's conversion follows her declaration and the revelation of Kuan-yin in splendour. In effect, the concrete physical sacrifice carries a double value: it repays the filial debt both by relieving a father's suffering and by leading his darkened spiritual understanding towards enlightenment.

Miao-shan's filial response to parental love was picked out as an outstanding achievement of Kuan-yin in one of the thirteenth-century references quoted above, and this clue to her larger appeal in the Chinese world is vital. The reunion of filial daughter and contrite father is essential to the conclusion of the story in every version we know. Indeed, the paradox by which the rebellious, independent youngest daughter turns out the most filial of them all is the same in the 'kernel story' itself and in that larger international literature of like-minded tales. The developed legend of Miao-shan has refashioned this keystone of the narrative into a form which reconciles the ideals of Buddhist orthodoxy with those of Chinese secular society.

3. Miao-shan in the world of the dead

IN its second stage of development, Miao-shan's career follows a pattern which we can explain neither by discovering an appeal to those oppressed by married life, nor by pointing out a characteristically Buddhist way of repaying the inbred parental debt. In both these cases the story operates thematically on a human level, resolving human problems through (admittedly remarkable) human means. But Miao-shan's visit to Hell, her act of deliverance, her revival and transfiguration as the Bodhisattva Kuan-yin oblige us to take account of the divine breaking into the human world.

What the story offers on this new level is a sequence in which a young girl first separates herself from the destiny of her family, is rejected and embraces death; in the world of the dead she performs an act of catholic deliverance; then she returns to her former body, now bearing the divine name of Kuan-yin;[199] in her renewed earthly existence she eventually achieves a reconciliation with her father and family, and at the moment of reunion affirms her divine identity in a public transfiguration. I will suggest that on this level the story follows a sequence of stages analagous to those defined by Arnold van Gennep in his famous book *Les rites de passage*.[200]

The concept, familiar in general anthropological usage, is of a complex of rites used in many societies to convey individuals through their critical transitions from one social status to another. The characteristic pattern subdivides into '*rites of separation, transition rites,* and *rites of incorporation*', although it is understood that emphasis shifts between these groups according to circumstances.[201] In effect, the individual must first be ritually separated from his original social group; he then spends a period in a socially anomalous status which represents the heart of the transitional process; finally, he is ritually brought back into society, reincorporated in his new status.

Let us take this sequence as a formal framework and measure against it the story of Miao-shan. We find the story recording a transition by which an ordinary human being departs from her status in the parent society and eventually arrives at a status and role which mediate between the human order and the divine. This formulation comes close to defining the role of a priest. And the story itself — particularly in the play *Hsiang-shan chi* — identifies a priestly function more precisely with its description of what happens during Miao-shan's visit to the Underworld. She witnesses the sufferings of the souls in each compartment of Hell and in compassion performs for them a service of deliverance. With the accomplishment of this act, which we shall examine below, she is ready to assume her new status. She re-enters the living world and rejoins her family, but now on a new basis.

The suggestion of a priestly role leads us to look more closely at the chapter in which van Gennep considers rites of initiation — those associated with sexual maturity, with admission to religious fraternities, to secret societies, to the mystery cults of the ancient Mediterranean world, to the established religions of Asia and Europe.[202] We find that in many societies such rites simulate a death to the old life, an interval spent in a remote, other-worldly quarter (sometimes Hell itself), where privileged knowledge is imparted, and a rebirth into the human world, now in the new social capacity. The ordeals, physical isolation, appearance of death, descent to Hell and revival that characterise the ritual complex of initiation in many social and religious systems — these are ritual symbols which seem clearly echoed in the experiences of Miao-shan.

There is an important distinction to be observed between an actual ritual situation and the mythology which gives it authority. We must be clear that in the story of Miao-shan we are dealing with something of a mythological character. To interpret this in terms of a form which is ritually significant is not the same as identifying it with a public rite in actual social practice. The interpretation refers to mythological events which at most echo the symbolic experiences enacted in ritual. But it happens that Miao-shan's visit to the world of the dead does reflect a ritual situation which does much to clarify its significance. In traditional Chinese society the act of delivering souls in Hell was and is a priestly function of great importance. Although the Buddhist monastic community was increasingly a despised class in the eyes of secular Chinese society in the post-Sung era, there cannot have been many families who did not feel it necessary or desirable to engage the professional services of monks in performing the essential ceremonies for the safe deliverance of their dead. These ceremonies have been the most significant point of contact between the Buddhist Saṅgha and the community at large.[203] And not only Buddhists are involved: the mourning services for the dead constitute a ritual complex in which Taoist and other religious groups can also make professional contributions. The various individual ceremonies can be performed in different versions according to the religious affiliations of the priests engaged.[204] But the ceremony most frequently performed in a Buddhist format is the Feeding of Hungry Ghosts,[205] and it is precisely in this rite that the canonical role of Kuan-yin is most conspicuous.

Kuan-yin is one of a large mythological company, spread through many cultures, who perform the exploit of going to Hell to save the damned. In Chinese Buddhist tradition it is a role shared also by Ti-tsang (Kṣitigarbha), the bodhisattva for whom the Underworld is a permanent abode. He presents a challenge to the absolute and undeniable justice of the King of Hell: in a quarter where the laws of retribution exact their due, this saviour is yet able to confound them through his powerful compassion.[206] Kuan-yin came to China already possessing the same property. The *Lotus sūtra* offered the faithful an assurance that to think upon the power of Kuan-yin would bring deliverance from 'all the evil states of existence, hells, ghosts and animals'.[207] The *Kāraṇḍavyūhasūtra* gave a more explicit account of how Kuan-yin entered and moved gloriously through the Avīci hell, transforming it into a paradise, then turned to the Citadel of the Hungry Ghosts, quenched its fires, gave the inmates food and drink, and led them to rebirth in the paradise Sukhāvatī.[208]

These teachings have profoundly influenced Chinese religious practice. Kuan-yin, like Ti-tsang, has for centuries been ritually enlisted when the souls of the newly dead have to be helped in their passage through the other world, particularly at the series of critical arraignments in the courts of Hell which culminate, on the forty-ninth day after death, with the moment of rebirth in a new existence. The filial duty of mourners through this period, and later on recurrent 'memorial' occasions, is to add to their deceased relatives' store of merit by various ritual means. The Feeding of Hungry Ghosts is designed to serve this end.

In Chinese usage the beings known as Hungry Ghosts share both the sufferings of the Buddhist *preta*, who roam through the world tortured by unrelievable hunger and thirst, and the wretched plight of the native Chinese 'Orphaned Souls' (*ku-hun*), deprived of sacrificial offerings and often of proper burial.

Interpretations

When at large, particularly during the seventh lunar month, they are liable to work vindictive damage in the world of men.[209] To feed, deliver and lead them through teaching to a higher existence generates merit which can be set to the account of particular souls. It thus enables mourners, with the help of qualified priests, to render their dead an important filial service. The ceremony occupies a central position not only in private post-mortuary and memorial services, but in the elaborate public rituals of the seventh month dedicated expressly to the relief of Orphaned Souls now let loose from their place in Hell: also an occasion for offerings of sustenance and merit to the souls of departed ancestors.

The roots of this ritual institution in Chinese life can be traced as a liturgical tradition back to the T'ang period and beyond. But the liturgies most widely used in modern times are the result of long editorial labours to discipline and refine an earlier complex of ritual practice. This process, spread over many stages from the eleventh to the seventeenth centuries,[210] runs parallel in time with the growth of the Miao-shan legend.

The colourful Tantric rite represented by the *fang-yen-k'ou* tradition dominates current Buddhist practice of the 'Hungry Ghosts' ceremony.[211] In it we find the situation explicitly and precisely represented.[212] During the preparatory stages of the rite the officiating priest formally puts on the five-pointed crown which signifies his identity with the Vairocana Buddha;[213] then, using the sacred elements of water and rice, and with prayers, invocations and *mudrās*, he creates a cosmos and assumes his central role in it. There comes a point[214] where he makes an offering of water to all the spiritual powers in the universe, asking for their protection and blessing on the relatives of the sponsor; then, uttering lines in celebration of Kuan-yin's saving power, he makes with his fingers the *mudrā* 'Entering the Kuan-yin meditation', and directs his mind intently upon the Bodhisattva. Emerging from this meditation, he repeats the *mudrā* and utters a passage ending with the line, 'My own person is indeed the same as Kuan-tzu-tsai' (i.e. Kuan-yin) — words which are firmly glossed by the seventeenth-century editor Chuhung as expressing the reality of a personal experience (親證親入也).[215] He is now ready to form the *mudrā* 'Breaking open Hell', which causes shafts of dazzling light to burst open the gates of Hell.[216] He utters the 'Bodhisattva vow' — 'I vow not to attain buddhahood until Hell is empty', invites the presence of Ti-tsang and other compassionate deities, then summons up all the ranks of Orphaned Souls, listing out their many stations in life and forms of untimely death. He proceeds with the absolution of their sins and ritual distribution of sacred food, finally directing them towards rebirth in Paradise.

In sum, the officiant formally assumes the identity of Kuan-yin. He releases and ministers to the Orphaned Souls in the person of the Bodhisattva. As a qualified priest he can renew again and again the saving annihilation of Hell pioneered by Kuan-yin. The Feeding of Hungry Ghosts thus presents a specific ritual parallel to the story of Kuan-yin's exploit in Hell. The story, for its part, serves as a mythological document explaining and validating the ritual actions of the priest. It is a 'charter' for the rite in the sense defined by Malinowski: in his words, it lays down 'the effective precedent of a glorified past for repetitive actions in the present'.[217]

The implications of all this for the story of Miao-shan are important, but need to be stated with care. The mythological authority for the 'Hungry Ghost' rites derives essentially from the canonical Bodhisattva Kuan-yin and his specific work of salvation in Hell. Miao-shan's career as a whole is not identical or interchangeable with this. But Miao-shan, as we can now see, brings together two distinct figures with a common purpose: the filial child of folk tradition becomes identified with the lofty, compassionate and all-powerful saviour of the damned; and in Chinese religious life the salvation of the damned is integral with the ritual practice of filial piety. The meeting of the two figures makes a double demand upon the story: it must identify each of them clearly, revealing their separate fields of action; it must also reconcile their basically different status in the spiritual and cosmic order. The framework of transition, which we have identified with the help of van Gennep's *rites de passage*, meets both demands simultaneously. As Miao-shan dies to her old life and awaits rebirth in the new, she performs the saving act which defines the essential character of her new status.

The meeting of two such persons in one is not unique in Chinese tradition. We know it well in the figure of Mu-lien. To the traditional Chinese world he is the filial child *par excellence*: the mortal son who reached the heights of spiritual perfection and from those heights battled with every difficulty to relieve and release his mother damned in Hell. Mu-lien too is a central figure in the *Yü-lan* rituals of the seventh month and in those parts of the Chinese mortuary ceremonies which deal with the safe passage of the dead through the Underworld. His credentials for these closely related functions are precisely his celebrated record as a mortal son who combines spiritual perfection and power with a passionate sense of filial piety.[218] The story of Miao-shan achieves the same for Kuan-yin. In place of the magnificent but impersonal figure who moved in state through the Avīci hell, we now see a young girl put ignominiously to death by her father, but who performs the same act of grace. The story gives a human face to the ideal of compassion and spiritual authority. And by bringing together the mortal filial child with the divine saviour, it pioneers a combination which is revived in ritual practice whenever children in mourning employ priests to perform the act of salvation on their departed parents' behalf.

4. *Concluding remarks*
THE argument of our last few pages can be summed up quite simply. We have found Miao-shan an exponent of filial piety on three distinct planes:
1. a physical plane — she succours her father in sickness by giving her arms and eyes as medicine;
2. a spiritual plane — she leads him to the true doctrine;
3. a ritual plane — she saves the Orphaned Souls in Hell and thus pioneers the meritorious action by which all filial children can serve the ritual needs of their parents' souls.
In each case her story is cognate with other Chinese and Buddhist legends of varying mythological and literary status.

The story also belongs to the specialised literature which affirms and defends the life of religious celibacy. Looking back now, we find that the schematic analogy of *rites de passage* — which underlies our 'ritual' interpretation above — can be used more generally to illuminate the careers of those pious women whose sufferings lead them through death and the Underworld to eventual rebirth and triumph. For they too achieve a new status by this means: beginning as oppressed, anti-social wives, they end as respected religious teachers. Whether or not the device of rebirth helps them in more practical ways (by making them male, gifted and successful), it always signals a formal change of status. Moreover, looking beyond these stories to those in which the women's sufferings stop short of death, we find the characteristic pattern of transition still latent, though less starkly expressed. Indeed, the 'first-stage' story of Miao-shan excellently illustrates how a difficult personal transition is achieved through separation, sojourn in a place remote from human society (here amid the solitude and rigours of Hsiang-shan), and final reintegration. The puzzling formal difference between first and second stages thus vanishes when we see the movement through death and rebirth as a transitional process different only in degree from the sequence of removal, isolation and rediscovery portrayed in the more earthbound stories. This formal analogy with *rites de passage* could be extended to embrace a wider range of mythological literature, and indeed a multitude of more subtle and ostensibly more secular situations in Chinese literature at large. Its purpose here, however, has now been adequately served.

It remains only to stress once more the versatility of the Miao-shan legend. Our discussion of 'interpretations' has singled out a few themes and implications of particular interest or difficulty. Taken as a whole, however, the texts we have studied show the story serving a wider range of needs and interests in Chinese society, and more would certainly emerge if the study were extended to include local traditions.

To the student the value of this story lies in its power of example. Simple in content, unsophisticated in literary form, accessible to historical and textual study (within the limits defined here), it enables us to form a rounded picture of how a legend could enter and establish itself in traditional currency. The forces at work on it can be seen reflected in the media which gave it that currency — popular devotional and liturgical literature, fiction, drama, balladry. Miao-shan's story may be relatively inconspicuous, but it does respond to study and analysis. Perhaps this example offers some hope that we can discover more coherence in that greater body of tradition which still seems so fragmented and problematical.

Notes

࿘࿘࿘࿘࿘࿘࿘࿘࿘࿘࿘࿘࿘࿘࿘࿘࿘࿘࿘࿘࿘

1. Introduction

1. Boxer (1953), p. 305.
2. Miguel de Loarca, *Verdadera relacion de la grandeza del reyno de China* (1575), part II, chapter 7. I am grateful to Professor van der Loon for drawing my attention to this source and for lending me his copy of Professor Boxer's transcript of this passage from MS. 2902 in the Biblioteca Nacional, Madrid; also to Mr. F.W. Hodcroft of Oxford University for clarifying certain points in the original Spanish.
3. *Historia de las cosas más notables, ritos y costumbres del gran Reyno de la China*, Rome 1585. For the relevant passage in the 1588 English version by Robert Parke, edited by Sir George T. Staunton, see Hakluyt Society First Series, vol. 14, 1853, pp. 41—2. On Mendoza's debt to the Loarca text, see Boxer (1953), pp. lxxix and lxxxix.
4. The legend has been regularly cited as a standard item in both specialised and popular accounts of Chinese mythology — see, for instance, de Groot (1886), pp. 188—97; Doré, pp. 94—138; Henri Maspero, 'Mythologie de la Chine moderne', in *Le taoïsme et les religions chinoises*, Paris 1971, pp. 191—2; Getty, pp. 83—4; E.T.C. Werner, *Myths and legends of China*, London 1922, pp. 253—87, and *A dictionary of Chinese mythology*, Shanghai 1932, p. 226.
5. Respectively by de Groot (1886), pp. 197—8, and Waley (1925). Both views, particularly the former, have been influential.
6. The outstanding contributions are by Yü Cheng-hsieh (*Kuei-ssu lei-kao*, 15.570—6), and Tsukamoto Zenryū. More recent studies by Yoshioka Yoshitoyo (1971) and Sawada Mizuho (1963, 1964) have concerned themselves with the story in the context of popular religious literature.

2. The Kuan-yin cult at Hsiang-shan ssu

7. For Chiang's career, see *Sung-shih*, 343.10a—12a. On 26 January 1100, after about a month in office as prefect of Ju-chou, he was transferred on to Ch'ing-chou: see *Hsü tzu-chih t'ung-chien ch'ang-pien*, 519.4b; *Sung-shih*, 343.12a. He would thus appear to have been posted to Ju-chou in the last days of 1099 or first days of 1100. This accords well

enough with the '12 January' date given by Chiang himself below, particularly if allowance is made for travelling time.

8. See the monograph on this subject by Kobayashi Taichirō, and Getty, pp. 68, 77, 93.

9. A parallel case exactly contemporary with the developments described below would be the Śākyamuni Pagoda of the Fo-kung ssu in Ying-hsien, Shansi, which dates from the year 1056, under the Liao dynasty. The position of the image in relation to the total structure is illustrated in *Chung-kuo chien-chu* 中國建築 , Wen-wu ch'u-pan-she, Peking 1957, p. 8, fig. 3 and plate 54. In Buddhist tradition there was a canonical distinction between the *stūpa* (塔), housing sacred relics, and the *caitya* (支提), which marked sites of religious significance or housed bodhisattva images and other sacred objects: see *Mahāsaṅghikavinaya (T.* 22, no. 1425), 33.498b. But in Chinese usage the distinction faded, and the word *t'a* could cover all these and other functions, including the memorial stelae of deceased monks: see Mochizuki, 4.3835b and 3837c. In the present case, where sacred relics play a role in the story of the 'Ta-pei' site, the word *t'a* will be rendered as '*stūpa*' when there is specific reference to the conservation of relics, and 'pagoda' in other cases where the reference is less precise.

10. *Ta-Ming i-t'ung ming-sheng chih* (1630), Honan section, 12.11b; *Ho-nan t'ung-chih* (1869), 50.26b; Kobayashi, 21, pp. 89b, 99b; 22, pp. 5b—6b.

11. 'Tz'u-shou yüan-chu Chung-hai shang-jen ling-t'a chih', *Pao-feng hsien-chih* (1797), 15.4b—5a. The inscription stood upon a memorial stele to Chung-hai as the late superior of the Tz'u-shou yüan, one of a group of eight stelae later observed in the south-west corner of the Po-ch'üeh ssu (see below) by Po Hung. Po's critical study of the history of this monastery, 'Po-ch'üeh ssu k'ao', dated 1611, was reprinted in the same edition of the gazetteer (10.2a—4a). He was sceptical of a claim seen elsewhere in local records that the monastery was founded by a nun in 1072, and based much of his own discussion on the epigraphy available in its precincts. He pointed out the existence of two weather-beaten stone tablets bearing very early dates (553 and 559), but not without suspicious features. He found no evidence intervening in the long period before the inscription of 1051 under discussion here, and was finally unable to suggest a firm date for the monastery's foundation.

12. The reference sounds for the first time an ambiguity in the name of the site which continued to be of consequence. Hsiang-shan, the 'Incense Mountain', is a name often met in early Chinese Buddhist texts: cf. Yoshioka (1971), p. 126, n. 8. It was 'one of the ten fabulous mountains known to Chinese Buddhism, located in the region of the Anavatapta lake in Tibet; also placed in the Kunlun range' (W.E. Soothill and L. Hodous, *A dictionary of Chinese Buddhist terms*, Oxford 1937, p. 319). In the Ju-chou and Pao-feng records the name clearly belongs to a monastery, known as the 'Hsiang-shan ssu'. Buddhist monasteries in China were frequently associated by name with mountains, as explained in Welch (1967), p. 467, n. 4: 'The word *shan* was used to mean a mountain or mountains, island or islands, but in particular the principal monastery located there-

on ... The Ch'i-hsia Ssu is known as Ch'i-hsia Shan — although the mountain on which it stands is named She Shan', which 'testifies to the strength of the tendency to think of the monastery itself as a mountain.' In the present case the name Hsiang-shan enabled the pious to accord the site a dual status: it was both a real monastery which pilgrims could visit, and also a holy mountain whose geographical location could, as the legend developed, move at will about the country, or remain completely indeterminate.

13. *Pao-feng hsien-chih* (1837), 15.15b; *Ho-nan t'ung-chih* (1869), 50.26b; cf. the map in *Pao-feng hsien-chih* (1797), 2.8b, reproduced on the endpaper at the beginning of this volume.

14. See Po Hung's essay, *Pao-feng hsien-chih* (1797), 10.2b. A later piece by Li Hung-chih, undated but reprinted in the 1837 edition of *Pao-feng hsien-chih* (15.15b—17a), pointed out that the association with Miao-shan had kept the monastery still flourishing through the ages, although like most such establishments it had passed through many vicissitudes.

15. *Ju-chou ch'üan-chih* (1840), 10.45a, in an essay by Liu Jo-tsai commemorating a later restoration of the Kuan-yin Pagoda. Liu's work is undated, but he speaks of 'more than six hundred years' having passed since the foundation in 1068. See also *Ho-nan t'ung-chih* (1869), 50.26b.

16. *Pao-feng hsien-chih* (1797), 15.6b—7a.

17. For Fan's activity as a painter of Ta-pei images in Szechuan monasteries in the mid-ninth century, see Kobayashi, 22, p. 5.

18. *Hua-p'in*, 1b. Li Chien's biography in *Sung-shih*, 444.8b, tells how after the death of Su Shih in 1101, deeply afflicted, 'he travelled about the region of Hsü (in central Honan) and Ju'. He may thus have visited the Hsiang-shan site at that late stage in his life, after the crucial visit of Chiang Chih-ch'i. For a discussion of the painting at Hsiang-yang, see Kobayashi, 22, pp. 5b—6b.

19. Equivalent to 12 January 1100.

20. 'Ju-chou Hsiang-shan Ta-pei p'u-sa chuan', *Pao-feng hsien-chih* (1797), 15.7a—8a. The offices and titles associated in the inscription with Chiang Chih-ch'i and Ts'ai Ching correspond to those recorded at this point in their official biographies (*Sung-shih*, 343.12a and 472.1b—2a). Chiang was restored to imperial favour and high office with the accession of the emperor Hui-tsung, who succeeded Che-tsung upon the latter's death in February 1100 (*Sung-shih*, 18.15b).

21. Chu evidently has in mind such passages as that concerning Avalokiteśvara's thirty-two manifestations in the tenth-century version of *Śūraṅgamasūtra* (*T*. 19, no. 945), 6.128b—129a; his second reference is to some work from the large body of esoteric texts concerned with the rituals and iconography of the Ta-pei cult translated in the course of the T'ang dynasty: see Kobayashi, 20, pp. 6 ff.

22. *Ch'ü-Wei chiu-wen*, 6.6ab. Cf. *Ch'in-ting ssu-k'u ch'üan-shu tsungmu*, 121.1a—2a, pointing out passages in the work which indicate that it was written at least ten years after the beginning of the author's period of captivity in the north (from 1127 to 1144): hence perhaps between 1137 and 1144. The passage in question here was first pointed out by Yü

Cheng-hsieh, *Kuei-ssu lei-kao*, 15.570.

23. For an important part of his career, beginning in 624, Tao-hsüan worked in various monasteries in the area of Chung-nan shan, a range stretching through southern Shensi, also known as 'Nan-shan'. His association with the area was so close that he and his sect were known by the name 'Nan-shan'. See Mochizuki, 4.3882c.

24. His *Chi Shen-chou san-pao kan-t'ung lu*, written in a Chung-nan shan monastery in 664, assembles traditions concerning many Buddhist sites, but the Hsiang-shan ssu is not included. His *Tao-hsüan Lü-shih kan-t'ung lu*, dating from the same year, is written in the form of questions and answers between Tao-hsüan and informants from the other world, and likewise records information concerning sacred sites. Here too the Hsiang-shan story is lacking. Cf. Tsukamoto, p. 267.

25. Tsukamoto, p. 271. On the economic livelihood of the Wu-t'ai shan complex, see Edwin O. Reischauer, *Ennin's travels in T'ang China*, New York 1955, pp. 207—11. On Mañjuśrī, see Lamotte (1960).

26. The three missing characters are in a position to modify the phrase *tao-ch'ang* 道場. Since this is often used to designate a place in which enlightenment is attained, it seems likely that the missing passage originally alluded to Miao-shan's enlightenment.

27. 現相□跡. The missing character may have been 示, by analogy with the phrase 示跡 used again in the same connection later in the same inscription: *Pao-feng hsien-chih* (1797), 16.6a.

28. 大士遺身. The term '*ta-shih*' is a standard translation of the Sanskrit *Mahāsattva*, 'Great Being', and can be associated specifically with Kuan-yin. Helen B. Chapin has discussed an instance in Yünnanese tradition of the term implying an appearance of Kuan-yin in human form: see her 'Yünnanese images of Avalokiteśvara', *Harvard Journal of Asiatic Studies* 8, 1944—5, pp. 151—3. Cf. Edouard Chavannes, 'Bulletin critique: Sainson, *Nan-tchao ye-che*', *T'oung Pao*, S.2, 5, 1904, p. 480. The term '*i-shen*' is one of several standard renderings of the Sanskrit *śarīra*, and designates the preserved human remains of holy beings treated as objects of veneration: see Mochizuki, 3.2185c ff.

29. In the popular calendar the birthday of Kuan-yin is celebrated on the 19th of the second month. Other days dedicated to Kuan-yin in the same month are listed by Tsukamoto, p. 263.

30. 'Ch'ung-chien Ju-chou Hsiang-shan Kuan-yin ch'an-yüan chi', *Pao-feng hsien-chih* (1797), 16.4a—6b. The extract quoted falls on 16.4b. This inscription describes the circumstances in which the monastery, apparently totally laid waste around the year 1184, was rebuilt through the patronage of a Jurchen princess, daughter of the Chin emperor Shih-tsung, and her husband Ta T'ien-hsi. The author, whose name is largely effaced in the inscription, resembles Chiang Chih-ch'i in his sense of personal response to words contained in the original text attributed to Tao-hsüan. The passage he quotes is unfortunately defective, but the fragmentary opening words run: 'The traces left on earth by a holy one are subject to (?) rise and fall in their fortunes...' 聖人示跡興廢有□□ □□年當重□□ (16.6ab). The closing phrases appear to correspond to the passage quoted by Chiang Chih-ch'i.

31. *Shao-shih shan-fang pi-ts'ung*, 40.537—8; *Kuei-ssu lei-kao*, 15.570; Tsukamoto, pp. 267—71.

32. The local gazetteers contain scattered references to building and restoration activities at different periods, as well as reproducing various commemorative texts in honour of deceased abbots. Some dates in the history of the Po-ch'üeh ssu are: 1382, 1559 (full or partial restorations: see *Pao-feng hsien-chih* (1797), 10.1b—2a); 1630 (extension to buildings: see ibid., 10.4a); the monastery was destroyed during the troubles at the end of the Ming, partially rebuilt in the early Ch'ing, restored some eighty years later (*Pao-feng hsien-chih* (1837), 15.16ab). Less clear information is available on the Hsiang-shan ssu from the time of its first destruction and restoration in 1184—5 (see above, n. 30), down to the seventeenth century, when the monastery was restored in the opening years of a new emperor's reign — most probably K'ang-hsi, in 1662—3 (see above, n. 15).

33. See above, n. 14. For the appearance of the Po-ch'üeh ssu in the story, see below, ch. 3.2. The connection was taken with such seriousness locally that Po Hung devoted much of his critical essay on the monastery to a detailed and sceptical analysis of the false historical questions raised (*Pao-feng hsien-chih* (1797), 10.2b—4a).

3. Versions of the story to 1500

34. By 'legend' is understood: a traditional tale which addresses an appeal to the beliefs of its hearers. In terms of this working definition Miao-shan's story begins to be a legend when it 'takes on a life of its own', and begins to lose its legendary quality when treated in such a way that its receivers no longer care whether it is true or not.

35. Sawada Mizuho, 'Hōken to Bukkyō setsuwa', pp. 191—3; (1965), pp. 79—83.

36. The dating is based on an entry in an early fourteenth-century Buddhist compilation, the *Fo-tsu li-tai t'ung-tsai*, 20.691a. Although Tsu-hsiu's title appears there in a slightly modified form, the same work must presumably be meant (Mochizuki, 5.4993c).

37. *Lung-hsing Fo-chiao pien-nien t'ung-lun*, 13.277b—278b.

38. Tsukamoto, p. 271.

39. Yoshioka Yoshitoyo has argued (1966) that the *Chin-kang k'o-i*, still in circulation and liturgical use as a work of the *pao-chüan* type (see below, ch. 3.5), dated originally from the thirteenth century. For the passage in question here, see *Hsiao-shih chin-kang k'o-i hui-yao chu-chieh*, 1.129ab.

40. Only the queen's name — Pao-ying in one, Pao-te in the other — strikes a jarring note; but this single minor discrepancy scarcely presents a serious problem in texts which bear several signs of graphic corruption.

41. In fact the remains of a Han township, Fu-ch'eng hsien, lay a few miles to the north-east of the Hsiang-shan ssu, close to the Po-ch'üeh ssu: see *Pao-feng hsien-chih* (1797), 2.8b. In his essay on the latter Po Hung considered and rejected the possibility that the king who was Miao-shan's father could be identified as a Han prince (ibid., 10.3ab).

42. Hsing-hsiu's preface (226a—227a) is dated 1223. Biographical references to him are accurately summarised in Mochizuki, 1.592c.

43. For an examination of the dating and literary context of this and similar works, see Patrick Hanan, 'Sung and Yüan vernacular fiction: a critique of modern methods of dating', *Harvard Journal of Asiatic Studies* 30, 1970, pp. 166—7.

44. *Hsin-pien Tsui-weng t'an-lu*, 6.40. I read 報 in place of 救 as the verb in the final phrase, since only this seems to fit the object 恩 . The character 救 reappears immediately after this phrase and may have prompted a textual slip.

45. For a summary of evidence concerning this text, see G. Dudbridge, *The Hsi-yu chi, a study of antecedents to the sixteenth-century Chinese novel*, Cambridge 1970, pp. 25—9.

46. *Ta-T'ang San-tsang ch'ü-ching shih-hua*, 1.5b—6a; 1955 reprint, 16—17.

47. It will be seen that I do not agree with Ōta Tatsuo in identifying the monastery as the Hsiang-shan ssu at Lung-men in Honan with which Po Chü-i was associated (see Ōta Tatsuo, p. 143). The reference to the Thousand Arms and Eyes is surely evidence enough that the Ju-chou cult was at least at the back of the author's mind, even though his further remarks shift the monastery into uncertain and fabulous territory.

48. *Kuei-ssu lei-kao*, 15.570—6.

49. *Ch'a-hsiang shih ts'ung-ch'ao*, 13.3a; *Ch'a-hsiang shih hsü-ch'ao*, 17.2b—3a. For details of textual inconsistencies, see below, n. 51.

50. For a description of the *Lü-ch'uang nü-shih* and a brief discussion of its authorship, see Wang Chung-min and Yüan T'ung-li, *A descriptive catalog of rare Chinese books in the Library of Congress*, Washington 1957, pp. 763—4. For indirect references by Japanese scholars to the Kuan Tao-sheng text, see Tsukamoto Zenryū, pp. 270—1; Yoshioka Yoshitoyo (1971), p. 122; Sawada Mizuho, 'Hōken to Bukkyō setsuwa', p. 184.

51. One clear example is the phrase 'an old man fed her with mountain peaches' 山桃, in the reprint (1b—2a). Yü, citing this phrase verbatim (*Kuei-ssu lei-kao*, 15.574) has 'fairy peaches' 仙桃, an obviously preferable reading which indicates minor graphic corruption in the reprint. The name of Miao-shan's eldest sister is Miao-yin 妙因 in the reprint (1a), Miao-yin 妙音 in Yü's citation (15.572). Although these secondary names vary widely in different versions, the latter is met most frequently, in the Tsu-hsiu version and later, and has canonical overtones to be discussed further below. Yü Yüeh's quotation of the title and text of Kuan Tao-sheng's version corresponds in all particulars to the *Lü-ch'uang nü-shih* reprint, which he was no doubt using (although he too contrived to transcribe Miao-shan's own name mistakenly).

52. 'Wei-kuo fu-jen Kuan-shih mu-chih ming', *Sung-hsüeh chai wen-chi, wai-chi*, 18ab. She died on 29 May 1319.

53. *Lü-ch'uang nü-shih*, part 10. The item is separately paginated. Textual variants are given above in n. 51. The closing phrases are quoted by Yü Cheng-hsieh in a separate essay on the name Kuan-shih-yin: *Kuei-ssu lei-kao*, 15.577.

54. The most comprehensive and up-to-date surveys of *pao-chüan* material are by Li Shih-yü (1961) and Sawada Mizuho (1963). On the social and religious context of *pao-chüan* literature, see especially

Yoshioka Yoshitoyo (1952), ch. 1; Sakai Tadao, ch. 7; Li Shih-yü (1957).

55. For instance by de Groot (1903), pp. 176 ff.; Topley (1963); Sakai Tadao; Li Shih-yü (1957); Suzuki Chūsei (1943).

56. On popular Buddhist sectarian activity in the Sung, see Suzuki Chūsei (1941). As Tsukamoto has pointed out (p. 270), the names of several local religious groups in the Ju-chou area are handed down in the gazetteers: cf. *Pao-feng hsien-chih* (1797), 16.9a.

57. This question is explored by Sawada Mizuho in 'Hōken to Bukkyō setsuwa'.

58. Yoshioka (1971), pp. 122—3. One such reference has already been noted, in the *Chin-kang k'o-i* (above, ch. 3.2). Another similar reference is found in a rare work of the late twelfth century which I have not seen — the *Ju-ju yü-lu* 如如語錄 of which a 1386 reprint is preserved in a Kyoto monastery: see Yoshioka (1966), p. 170, n. 29.

59. One of the five cardinal scriptures attributed to Lo Ch'ing (1443?—1527), founding father of the system of sects which later bore his name (*Lo-chiao*). The 1509 edition of the *T'ai-shan pao-chüan* is reportedly in the collection of Fu Hsi-hua: see Li Shih-yü (1961), p. 50, no. 441. The 'Hsiang-shan' reference is noted by Yoshioka, who possessed the book briefly while in Peking during the Second World War: (1952), pp. 23 and 26. On the life of Lo Ch'ing, see Sawada (1951) and Yoshioka (1952), pp. 26—35; on the Lo sects, see *inter alia* Yoshioka (1952), pp. 36—43; Suzuki (1943); Sakai, pp. 468—80.

60. Li Shih-yü (1961), preface, pp. 10—11; Yoshioka (1952), p. 25.

61. Yoshioka (1971), pp. 129—94. References below to this edition will give the original Chinese pagination, not that of the reprint.

62. In the twelfth century and later this monastery became one of the principal Kuan-yin cult centres in China: see the account in Saeki Tomi, pp. 382—3.

63. It is also headed, like other editions of this work, by a celebratory preface claiming to date from the Sung period. The author is named as Hai-yin, attached to the Wu Residence, but no further details are given. Yoshioka Yoshitoyo once tentatively identified the royal patron as Chao Pi (d. 1106), Prince Jung-mu of Wu, ninth son of the Sung emperor Shen-tsung: (1952), p. 18; but later he left the question once again open: (1971), p. 124. Without real authentication the preface is of little use in establishing a date for the text we now have.

64. I am grateful to Professor B.L. Riftin of Moscow for pointing out the existence of a shorter work bearing the title *Hsiang-shan pao-chüan* which may also date from the eighteenth century. It is no. A—1439 in the Library of the Committee of Social Sciences, Hanoi, and is not listed in the standard *pao-chüan* catalogues.

65. Yoshioka (1971), p. 122.

66. One from P'u-t'o shan, dated 1878 (Cambridge University Library), the other dated 1908 (n.p.) (School of Oriental and African Studies).

67. He cites several of the self-styled 'reprint' editions of the nineteenth and twentieth centuries listed in various sources: Yoshioka (1971), pp. 118—9; cf. Cheng Chen-to (1963), 5.76a; Fu Hsi-hua,

pp. 47—8; Tsukamoto Zenryū, p. 265; Li Shih-yü (1961), pp. 56—7; Sawada Mizuho (1963), pp. 107—9.

68. Yoshioka (1971), p. 122 and p. 126, n. 3.
69. Cf. P.D. Hanan, 'The text of the *Chin P'ing Mei*', *Asia Major*, New Series, 9, 1962, p. 30.
70. *Ming-shih*, 74.1802; *Ch'in-ting Ta-Ch'ing hui-tien*, 85.15a. The correct written form of *ming-tsan* was 鳴贊. The *pao-chüan* text gives an inaccurate phonetic equivalent.
71. Sawada Mizuho (1956).
72. See, for instance, the titles and editions listed by Li Shih-yü (1961), pp. 56—7, and Yoshioka (1971), pp. 117—9.
73. *Ch'ien-tao Lin-an chih*, 3.29b; *Sung-shih*, 343.12a. The date of Chiang's appointment was first remarked by Sawada Mizuho: 'Hōken to Bukkyō setsuwa', p. 185.
74. For example, the scene in which Miao-shan is prepared for execution: the invocation breaks in six times within less than three full pages (55a—57b).
75. Katō Bunnō, p. 412.
76. 'Lung-shu' is a standard rendering of the Sanskrit name Nāgārjuna; Ju-chou was a real place, as seen above; 'Ch'eng-hsin', not recorded as a *hsien*-name, is a phrase of purely religious significance; Hui-chou was and is a city in Kwangtung.
77. Such terms as *Lung-hua hui* 龍華會 (23b), *wu-wei* 無為 (24a), *chen-k'ung* 真空 (71b), although not unknown to canonical Buddhism, had particular significance in sectarian religions: cf. Topley (1963), p. 373; Suzuki (1943), pp. 460 ff.; Li Shih-yü (1957), p. 172; Yoshioka (1952), p. 28; de Groot (1903), pp. 197 ff.; Sawada (1951).
78. For an illustration of this practice, which derives from the standard Buddhist meritorious action of reproducing sacred texts, see the many names of donors printed on the page-fold *passim* in the *Hsiang-shan pao-chüan* of Yoshioka's collection.

4. The sixteenth and seventeenth centuries
79. It was available to both de Groot and Doré when preparing their accounts of the Miao-shan story: see below, n. 89.
80. Sun K'ai-ti (1957), p. 177; Liu Hsiu-yeh, p. 86; Liu Ts'un-yan, pp. 215—7. An edition of 1819 in one *chüan* is listed in the collection of the Institute of Oriental Studies, Soviet Academy of Sciences: see *Katalog fonda kitaiskikh ksilografov Instituta Vostokovedeniya A.N.S.S.S.R.*, Moscow 1973, vol. 2, p. 328, no. 2647. For the sake of easy recognition the work is referred to here and below by its familiar title, although this is not attested by early bibliographical evidence. In textual references the abbreviation '*Nan-hai*' will be used.
81. As at the opening of *chüan* 1. There are small variants in later *chüan*.
82. For details, see Dudbridge (1969), p. 157, n. 66.
83. Sun K'ai-ti (1957), p. 138: the *Yü-lou ch'un* 玉樓春. I have not seen this edition and simply record Sun's dating.
84. For examples of work published under this name, see Sun K'ai-ti

(1957), pp. 28, 34, 35, 42, 50, 169; Dudbridge (1969), pp. 146, 147, 149.

85. For details of these editions, see in order: 1. W.L. Idema, 'Some remarks and speculations concerning p'ing-hua', T'oung Pao, S.2, 60, 1974, p. 152; 2. Sun K'ai-ti (1958), pp. 51—2; 3. Sun K'ai-ti (1957), p. 171, and Chou Yüeh-jan, pp. 89—92, 160—1; 4. Liu Ts'un-yan, pp. 4—5, 202—3; 5. ibid., p. 188; 6. Sawada Mizuho, 'Daruma-den shōsetsu'; 7. Sun K'ai-ti (1957), p. 170; 8. Dudbridge (1969), p. 157; 9. Sun K'ai-ti (1957), p. 169; 10. ibid., p. 112; 11. ibid.; 12. Sun K'ai-ti (1958), p. 141, and Li T'ien-i, p. 78; 13. Dudbridge, pp. 155—6. Details of all but nos. 3, 6 and 12 have been checked from the originals or from microfilm copies.

86. *Che-ku-t'ien*. The same tune opens the first scene of the play *Hsiang-shan chi* described below. In the two works of fiction the 'tune' is a token title fitted to passages in lines of five syllables (*Nan-hai*) and seven syllables (*Chung K'uei*).

87. Dudbridge (1969).

88. Studies of early *Hsi-yu chi* editions dealing in part with the position of Chu's version have been published by Ōta Tatsuo: see in particular *Kōbe gaidai ronsō* 19.1, 1968, p. 32; 20.3—4, 1969, pp. 13—22; 21.1—2, 1970, pp. 1—10.

89. de Groot (1886), p. 197. Both de Groot and Doré based their extended accounts of the Miao-shan story on this text, the latter using an illustrated edition of 1819 (Doré, p. 94, n. 1), the former 'un opuscule qui circulait à Makao à une époque où nous y séjournions'. Both accounts follow the text closely enough to make an identification possible, although both appear to misread some points of detail, and in de Groot's case the story sometimes takes a wayward turn. Some discrepancies may be due to textual variants. Doré's *illustrations* are from some other source and do not reflect the content of his text. Compare also the remarks by Maspero in 'Mythologie de la Chine moderne', *Le taoïsme et les religions chinoises*, Paris 1971, p. 191.

90. For the canonical origins of the attendant figures — the young pilgrim Sudhana and the daughter of Sāgara the dragon king — see Jan Fontein, *The pilgrimage of Sudhana*, The Hague 1967; Noël Peri, 'Hārītī la Mère-de-démons', ' *Bulletin de l'Ecole Française d'Extrême-Orient* 17.3, 1917, pp. 72—3. On illustrations of Kuan-yin in the Wan-li period, see *Shao-shih shan-fang pi-ts'ung*, 40.537; compare also *Chin P'ing Mei tz'u-hua*, 7.5b.

91. *Nan-hai*, 2.20a—21a; *Hsi-yu chi*, 98.1105. The plunge from a mountain height is one of the standard perils from which Kuan-yin guarantees deliverance in the *P'u-men p'in* section of the *Lotus sūtra*: see Katō Bunnō, p. 412.

92. *Nan-hai*, 2.21ab; cf. *T'ang San-tsang hsi-yu shih-o chuan* (item 7 in above list), 4.5b—8b; *Hsi-yu chi*, 9.90—1. Reasons for suspecting the insertion of the episode by Chu are set out in Dudbridge (1969), pp. 170—83. Dr. Anthony C. Yu in a recent article, 'Narrative structure and the problem of chapter nine in the *Hsi-yu chi*' (*Journal of Asian Studies* 34, 1975, 295—311), aligns himself with the Ch'ing editors of *Hsi-yu chi* in feeling that for internal reasons the story of Ch'en Kuang-jui should be regarded as integral with the hundred-chapter novel. I find that the arguments pro-

posed beg too many textual and literary questions to command acceptance, and consider that the weight of textual and literary evidence still lies on the side of the Ming editors who left us the best editions of the novel we possess, all lacking the narrative used by Chu Ting-ch'en for his 'Ch'en Kuang-jui' story. On the subject of dealings between men and magic fish in Chinese fiction, see P.D. Hanan, *The Chinese short story* (Harvard-Yenching Institute Monograph Series 21, Cambridge, Massachusetts, 1973), pp. 196—7. With his use of the 'Third Crown Prince' as the linking dragon in his 'Lung-nü' episode (*Nan-hai*, 2.21ab) the compiler recalls another well-known figure from the *Hsi-yu chi* — the grateful dragon rescued from torment by Kuan-yin and later recruited to serve Tripitaka: see *Hsi-yu chi*, 8.86, 15.171.

93. *Hsi-yu chi*, 77.888. In earlier Buddhist iconography the lion of Mañjuśrī is usually coloured white, although parts of him are sometimes green: see Waley (1931), pp. 54, 153, 216, 236—7, 250, 257, 265.

94. Danger from wild beasts is another of the standard perils listed in the *gāthās* of the *P'u-men-p'in* section of the *Lotus sūtra* (Katō, p. 413). Illustrators in India and China have represented these as lions and elephants: see Miyeko Murase, 'Kuan-yin as savior of men: illustration of the twenty-fifth chapter of the Lotus sūtra in Chinese painting', *Artibus Asiae* 33.1—2, 1971, p. 72, and Helen B. Chapin (1971), p. 76.

95. Ch'ing-liang shan was early identified with Wu-t'ai shan in Shansi, the major cult centre of Mañjuśrī. For the scriptural authority for this, see Waley (1931), pp. xxxix, 198. For a parallel reference to Ch'ing-liang shan in Ming fiction, see *Hua-kuang t'ien-wang chuan* (item 5 in list above), 3.10a—18a. The *Hsi-yu chi* (61.705) associates Ch'ing-liang tung with O-mei shan, the reputed home of Samantabhadra.

96. See the table of proper names in appendix below. Note that there are some exceptions, particularly the changed identities of certain celestial protectors and the different location of Hsiang-shan, now in fact identified with P'u-t'o shan.

97. The introduction of Shan-ts'ai and Lung-nü (after Miao-shan's arrival at Hsiang-shan) and the seditious scheme of the two sons-in-law (after the king has contracted his disease). The matching passages in the two works can be tabulated as follows:

Pao-chüan	: Nan-hai
18a—85a	: 1.11b—2.19b
86a—94b	: 3.1a—3.6b
96a—101a	: 3.10a—3.13a

98. *Pao-chüan*, 25a—26a; cf. *Nan-hai*, 1.13b—14a. This passage is unique in the novel for being an utterance in verse by a character in the story. In the *pao-chüan*, of course, such passages are commonplace.

99. For example, the abbess at the Po-ch'üeh ssu reveals to Miao-shan that the king has threatened to destroy their monastery if she will not return to marry (2.5a, cf. *pao-chüan*, 43b). But this punishment was not specified by the king at the time (2.1b), although it was in the *pao-chüan* (37a). The absence of one four-character phrase has made the difference here. For similar features in Chu Ting-ch'en's version of the *Hsi-yu chi*, see Dudbridge (1969), pp. 163 ff.

100. Patrick Hanan, 'The *Yün-men chuan*: from *chantefable* to short story', *Bulletin of the School of Oriental and African Studies* 36, 1973, 299—308: see in particular p. 306.

101. A straightforward example is the Cantonese *nan-yin* 南音 ballad *Kuan-yin ch'u-shih* 觀音出世, current until recently in a block-printed edition by the Wu-kuei t'ang 五桂堂 of Hong Kong. It reproduces almost slavishly the narrative content of the *Nan-hai Kuan-yin ch'üan-chuan*, although even here there are episodic departures — the recruitment of Shan-ts'ai, for instance, is identified with a *Hsi-yu chi* episode (chapters 40—42) in which the demon Hung-hai-erh is defeated by Kuan-yin and given this new name.

102. Such a standard work in its own time as Getty (1928) accepted this version as authoritative (pp. 83—4).

103. See Sakai Tadao, pp. 251—7.

104. *Chi-ku-ko chen-ts'ang pi-pen shu-mu*, 16a.

105. See *Naikaku bunko Kanseki bunrui mokuroku*, 285b. A copy of this edition dated 1607 is reprinted (but without illustrations) in *Tao-tsang*, fasc. 1105—6. The work will be referred to below as *Tseng-pu sou-shen chi*. Lo Mao-teng, of whom virtually nothing is known, is regarded as the author of the novel *Hsi-yang chi* 西洋記, and his name is associated with the Ming play *Hsiang-shan chi* discussed below. His preface to the present work speaks of acquiring the book from the Fu-ch'un t'ang on a visit to Nanking in 1593: the book may thus have appeared before this date.

106. For examples of early editions, see *Naikaku bunko Kanseki bunrui mokuroku*, 287b; Sakai Tadao, pp. 299 ff. Page references below are to the Yeh Te-hui reprint, referred to as *San-chiao yüan-liu*.

107. Li Hsien-chang, pp. 79—83.

108. *Tseng-pu sou-shen chi*, first item in *chüan* 3.

109. *San-chiao yüan-liu*, 4.10a—11b.

110. See the comparative table of proper names in appendix below.

111. *San-chiao yüan-liu*, 4.10b; *Nan-hai*, 2.13b—14a; contrast *pao-chüan*, 71ab.

112. *San-chiao yüan-liu*, 4.11a (*p'i-mao chih yü* 披毛之語); *Nan-hai*, 2.17a (*p'i-mao chih hua* 披毛之話); contrast *pao-chüan*, 80ab.

113. *San-chiao yüan-liu*, 4.11b; *Nan-hai*, 4.17ab.

114. A strange exception is found at the point where the queen intercedes for Miao-shan at the last moment before her execution. It is suggested in the text that the queen is motivated by the hope that Miao-shan will marry and take over the reins of power. In its interest in motivation for its own sake and its adumbration of a development in the story which can never take place, this feature is remarkably out of harmony with the narrative conventions in which the Miao-shan story is usually treated.

115. For example: when the Po-ch'üeh ssu begins to burn, Miao-shan draws blood to spit towards the sky by biting her finger, not stabbing her lip (contrast *pao-chüan*, 51b; *Nan-hai*, 2.8a); the commander makes three attempts to burn the monastery, all of which fail (contrast *pao-chüan*, 52ab; *Nan-hai*, 2.8a).

116. Hsiung Lung-feng's name is familiar to students of Chinese fiction as the publisher of four vernacular stories and of a *Hsi-hsiang chi* edition dated 1592: see Ma Yau-woon (1968), pp. 258—60. In the credits of the *T'ien-fei niang-ma chuan* Hsiung describes himself as a book-dealer of Chien-yang (潭邑書林). (For the identification of 'T'an-i' as Chien-yang, see van der Loon's note in Dudbridge (1969), p. 155, n. 54.) For a description of the *T'ien-fei niang-ma chuan*, see Li Hsien-chang, pp. 91—7. A specimen page is illustrated in *Min-Shin sōzuhon zuroku* 明清插圖本圖錄, Tokyo 1942, plate 27, cf. text, p. 7; it is reproduced again in A-ying (1957), plate 16, cf. text, p. 5.

117. In the latter case because the publisher's *Hsi-hsiang chi* bears that date (Li, p. 92); (the 'Wan-li 30' date given by Li on p. 86 is presumably a misprint). In the former case the reason for the 1592 date (Li, p. 89) is not made clear.

118. Dudbridge (1969), p. 157, n. 66.

119. Thirty-two extant works in this series, showing a high degree of uniformity in style of publication, are listed in Nagasawa Kikuya (1936), pp. 5—6.

120. See *Ch'ü-hai tsung-mu t'i-yao*, 18.856; Sun K'ai-ti (1957), p. 59.

121. In *Ku-pen hsi-ch'ü ts'ung-k'an*, Second Series.

122. *Yüan-shan t'ang ch'ü-p'in*, 112.

123. Apart from certain changes in the names of minor characters (see table in appendix below), the following points are worth noting in passing: Miao-shan goes to a nunnery named Ch'ing-hsiu an, distinct from the nearby male monastery Po-ch'üeh ssu, and the king uses the compromising proximity of the two as his pretext for burning them both down; in due course both monks and nuns have thus to be delivered from Hell; the temptation of Miao-shan by the Buddha disguised as an eligible bachelor takes place here as an episode during her stay at the nunnery; her major trial at the nunnery is ordained by the king — she must prepare a vast vegetarian feast for the entire community — and in this too she is aided by spirits.

124. See, *inter alia*, Cheng Ch'ien, pp. 440—1; Ch'ien Nan-yang, pp. 5—6; Wang Ch'ing-cheng, p. 61.

125. The edition provides for nineteen such illustrations distributed through thirty scenes, although four are left blank in the second *chüan*.

126. Most conspicuously in sc. 18 (text), which covers the action represented by sc. 17—20 in the list of contents. Sc. 21—3 in the text match sc. 23—4 in the list of contents.

127. Sawada Mizuho, 'Shakkyōgeki joroku', p. 32.

128. The fact that the scenes in the text are numbered but not named may in itself reflect an earlier convention: cf. Cheng Ch'ien, p. 440.

129. Sawada Mizuho ('Shakkyōgeki joroku', p. 32) also points out that the theatrically required *sheng* 生 role is deliberately introduced into the story in sc. 2.

130. The text on 2.13a has simply '*wai*' 外 . Since the only speaking characters previously introduced in this scene are the *tan* 旦 (i.e. Miao-shan) and Yama (also styled 'King' 王), it seems reasonable to assume that the dialogue between them continues, implying that Yama was played

by a *wai*, or supporting, actor.

131. In canonical Buddhism the 'Fifty-three Salutations' are associated with the young Sudhana's famous pilgrimage, which took him to visit in turn fifty-three spiritual authorities (cf. above, n. 90). But probably more relevant here is the list of fifty-three Buddha-names given in the *Kuan Yao-wang Yao-shang erh p'u-sa ching* (663c), whose devout recitation brings deliverance from sin. This list of fifty-three names, usually joined with another list of thirty-five to make a total of eighty-eight, is in regular liturgical use: see *Li pa-shih-pa fo hung-ming pao-ch'an*.

132. Sawada Mizuho, 'Shakkyōgeki joroku', p. 33.

133. His illustrations sometimes show what happens on the stage as such (1.1b), sometimes attempt an imaginative rendering of a scene (2.9a, 14a), sometimes show something that could pass as either (1.4a, 9a, 19a; 2.11b, 19a).

134. An example is the *luan-t'an* play *Ta Hsiang-shan* 大香山 (of which Professor van der Loon has kindly shown me a copy deriving from a local MS. version), which is said to have been performed annually on the fifteenth of the seventh lunar month (hence at the climax of the *Yü-lan* season of rituals for the Hungry Ghosts) in front of the Ch'ih-ch'ien lou 赤崁樓 in Tainan.

135. Loarca, *Verdadera relacion*, part II, chapter 3 (cf. above, n. 2).

136. There are some slight but interesting differences. According to Loarca, 'the Chinese relate that the monkeys came from the mountain and helped her', whereas both *pao-chüan* (48b) and *Nan-hai* (2.6b) lack the monkeys, who actually appear when Miao-shan later establishes herself on Hsiang-shan (*Nan-hai*, 2.19a). Loarca makes no mention of the inhabitants of the monastery dying in its flames — only the 'statues of the saints'. He has Miao-shan attempt suicide by stabbing herself with a silver hairpin, saved only by the interruption of a rainstorm, but in *pao-chüan* (51b—52a) and *Nan-hai* (2.8a) she uses a bamboo hairpin to draw blood from her lips, spits it towards the heavens and so calls down the heavy fall of red rain; cf. *Hsiang-shan chi*, 2.8a, and *San-chiao yüan-liu*, 4.10a, where she draws blood by biting her finger.

137. Boxer (1953), p. 213. On da Cruz, his journey and his book, see ibid., pp. lviii ff.

138. This took place in June 1973, at a temple dedicated to Kuan-kung in Tsuen Wan, Hong Kong.

139. See Getty, pl. XXIII and p. 59; Chapin, pl. 37, no. 93 (p. 78) and pl. 40, no. 102 (p. 86).

140. For a nineteenth-century description of such figures in ritual use in Amoy, see de Groot (1886), pp. 427—8. On the *Yü-lan* rituals, see below, ch. 6.3.

141. For brief details on Chang Ta-fu, see *Ch'ü-hai tsung-mu t'i-yao*, 21.1027; *Ch'ü-lu*, 5.10b; Pei-ying (1959), p. 276, n. 41. The text of the play in manuscript form is reproduced in *Ku-pen hsi-ch'ü ts'ung-k'an*, Third Series. It is discussed by Sawada Mizuho, 'Shakkyōgeki joroku', pp. 33—6.

142. Cheng Chen-to, 'Fo-ch'ü hsü-lu', p. 1072; cf. Fu Hsi-hua, pp. 47—8; Sawada Mizuho (1963), p. 109. Nineteenth-century copies

outside Asia are found, for instance, in the Oriental Institute of the Soviet Academy of Sciences (*Katalog*, Moscow 1973, no. 2084; see also B. Riftin, L. Kazakova and E. Stulova, review of Li Shih-yü (1961) in *Narody Azii i Afriki*, 1963, 1, p. 218); also a bibliographically similar, though slightly later (1870) edition in the British Library (15103.b.9). References below are to the latter.

143. Reprint, Taipei 1962, of a lithographic edition dated 1923, based on an earlier woodblock edition and originally published in Shanghai; typeset edition based in turn on this by Jui-ch'eng shu-chü, Taichung, reissued 1969.

144. See Henri Borel, *Kwan Yin, een boek van de goden en de hel*, Amsterdam [1897], pp. 15—31, 86—106. The work is identified on p. 16, n. 1. The opening pages of the first section present an almost literal translation from the beginning of the Chinese text. Occasional details, including names of minor characters, differ from available Chinese versions.

145. In the Shanghai lithographic reprint. No reign-mark appears at this point in the British Library copy.

146. See table of proper names in appendix below. But the author evidently had no interest in the adventurous episodes added in the novel.

147. Li Shih-yü (1957), pp. 172—3; de Groot (1903), ch. 6; Topley (1963), pp. 370 ff.

148. *Kuan-yin chi-tu pen-yüan chen-ching*, 1.10ab.

149. More explicit references are found *passim*, for instance in the opening passage of the work, where Kuan-yin appeals to Yao-ch'ih Chin-mu (ibid., 1.1b). On the varied terminology used in referring to Mother, see Topley (1963), p. 370, n. 4.

150. *Wu-cho* 五濁 : a term of Buddhist derivation, denoting five successive periods of decay in human affairs: see Mochizuki, 2.1259c ff. Its apparent reference to women in this context is a special application of the term.

151. *Kuan-yin chi-tu pen-yüan chen-ching*, 1.1b.

152. Ibid., 1.24b—25a.

153. This subject is explored at length and in detail in Topley (1958).

154. *Kuan-yin chi-tu pen-yüan chen-ching*, 1.19a—22b.

155. Waley (1925), p. 131.

5. Anatomy of the story

156. See K.K. Bhishagratna (trans.), *The Sushruta Samhita*, Varanasi 1963, 3 vols., 3.270 and 274. The disease is mentioned several times in Chinese Buddhist literature, but not in any context directly relevant to the present story: cf. *T*. 30.357c; 31.703b; 50.1007b; 54.987a and 1165c.

157. These latter phrases are specified by Chüeh-lien. They are reflected also in the *Hsiang-shan pao-chüan* (89—94). See appendix.

158. *Sui-shu*, 34.1047. I am grateful to Professor A.F.P. Hulsewé for pointing out a listing of the same title in *T'ung-chih*, 69.812b, specifying division into 20 *chüan*. We cannot however be sure that this twelfth-century reappearance of the title was not derived from the *Sui-shu* entry. The variant numbering of *chüan* is graphically insignificant enough to be

the result of textual corruption.

159. See Edouard Chavannes, *Cinq cents contes et apologues extraits du Tripiṭaka chinois*, Paris 1962, vol. 1, nos. 2, 4, 5; cf. vol. 4, pp. 85—9.

160. *T.* 3.128—30; reproduced in *T.* 53.153—4 and 655—6; also *T.* 4.447c—449a.

161. In the widely circulated illustrated handbook of the Underworld, *Yü-li chih-pao pien* 玉歷至寶編 (var. *p'ien* 篇), this virtuous act is illustrated in the seventh court of Hell, that of T'ai-shan wang. (On this text, see Lu Hsün, pp. 440—6, and Sawada Mizuho (1968), pp. 30—6.) See also Gustave Dumoutier, *Le rituel funéraire des Annamites*, Hanoi 1902, pp. 184, 214, 225. A characteristic example is cited from a family genealogy by Francis L.K. Hsu, *Under the ancestors' shadow*, London 1949, p. 230. Others can be found in local gazetteers.

162. Chüeh-lien version, 129b; cf. above, ch. 3.2.

163. Tsu-hsiu version, 278a; cf. above, ch. 3.2.

164. Katō, p. 386; cf. *T.* 9.54a; Kern, pp. 384—5.

165. Chüeh-lien version, 129b.

166. The name appears in this full form in the 1185 inscription at the Hsiang-shan ssu, and in Chüeh-lien's version. Elsewhere it is freely abbreviated.

167. Skt. Vimaladattā (Kern, p. 419), Ch. Ching-te 淨德 (*T.* 9.59c). Cf. Chüeh-lien version: Pao-te 寶德 .

168. *T.* 9.53c; Katō, pp. 384—5; Kern, pp. 382—3.

169. Katō, p. 400; *T.* 9.56a; Kern, p. 402.

170. *T.* 53.159bc. Miao-yen is used as a woman's name in *T.* 14.54c.

171. For example, *T.* 16.154a ('Miao-shan p'u-sa'). For other usages, see *T.* 25.443b; 53.283a; 54.1077b.

172. *Sui-shu*, 69.1608. The phrase occurs in an address to the emperor Kao-tsu in 602 by Wang Shao, seeking to demonstrate that the recently dead empress Wen-hsien had ascended to heaven.

173. *Kuei-ssu lei-kao*, 15.571.

174. Kern, p. xxxi.

175. On the sources and development of the 'Leir' story, see W. Perrett, 'The story of King Lear from Geoffrey of Monmouth to Shakespeare', *Palaestra* 35, Berlin 1904.

176. The sample consists of the tales listed in S. Thompson and W.E. Roberts, *Types of Indic oral tales*, (FF Communications no. 180, Helsinki 1960), no. 923B; and in W. Eberhard, *Typen chinesischer Volksmärchen* (FF Communications no. 120, Helsinki 1937), no. 193 ('Das Mädchen, das den Bettler heiratet'). In the former, 'Minaevim' should read 'Minaev'; in the latter, the reference under 'f' should read: 'Min-su Nr. 47'.

177. Stith Thompson (trans. and enlarged), *The types of the folktale, a classification and bibliography* (FF Communications no. 184, Helsinki 1964), p. 8.

178. Thompson and Roberts, pp. 115—6.

179. This question will be more closely examined below: ch. 6.3.

180. For a brief study of the association of tiger and peach with New Year and other rituals, see J.J.M. de Groot, *The religious system of China*,

vol. 6, Leiden 1910, pp. 953—64.

6. Interpretations

181. See above, ch. 3.2 and n. 39.

182. Maurice Freedman, *Rites and duties, or Chinese marriage* (Inaugural lecture, London School of Economics and Political Science, London 1967), pp. 7 ff. For an extended account of the orthodox life-cycle of women in a traditional Chinese community, see Margery Wolf, *Women and the family in rural Taiwan*, Stanford 1972.

183. Cf. above, ch. 4.5 and n.152.

184. *Liu Hsiang pao-chüan*, 4b—6a. The original passage, framed as a public sermon by a nun named Chen-k'ung, is mostly in verse.

185. Typical cases, both influenced by the text cited above, are cited by Chou Tso-jen in his essay 'Liu Hsiang nü' (1937).

186. Cantonese-speaking establishments of this kind were the subject of Dr. Marjorie Topley's field study: Topley (1954), (1958).

187. Topley (1958), pp. 167 ff.

188. *Chin P'ing Mei tz'u-hua*, 33.2b; 39.14a—19b; 51.17a—19b; 73.8b—14b; 74.11a—17b; 82.5ab. The texts involved are analysed by Sawada Mizuho (1956).

189. *Chin P'ing Mei tz'u-hua*, 74.13a—17a. The story also survives in various modern *pao-chüan* versions: see Sawada (1956), p. 93, also (1963), pp. 142—3.

190. Some examples: *Liu Hsiang nü pao-chüan* (eighteenth and nineteenth-century editions, but known in the early seventeenth century: see Li Shih-yü (1961), pp. 27—8; Sawada Mizuho (1963), pp. 139 ff.; Cheng Chen-to, 'Fo-ch'ü hsü-lu', pp. 1087—8); *Hsiu-nü pao-chüan* 秀女寶卷 (nineteenth and early twentieth-century editions: cf. Li, p. 55; Cheng, p. 1092; Sawada, pp. 224—5); *Miao-ying pao-chüan* 妙英寶卷 (nineteenth and twentieth-century editions: Li, p. 32; Cheng, pp. 1086—7; Sawada, pp. 144—5); *Yü-ying pao-chüan* 玉英寶卷 (nineteenth and twentieth-century editions: Li, p. 62; Sawada, pp. 145—7); *Mei-shih pao-chüan* 梅氏寶卷 (modern editions: Li, p. 31, Topley (1958), pp. 373—4).

191. The story of the devout princess Nangsa: see L.A. Waddell, *The Buddhism of Tibet, or Lamaism*, second edn., reprinted Cambridge 1959, pp. 553—65; Jacques Bacot, *Trois mystères tibétains: représentations théâtrales dans les monastères du Tibet*, Paris 1921, pp. 229—96; Marion H. Duncan, *Harvest festival dramas of Tibet*, Hong Kong 1955, pp. 176—271; Wang Hsiao, *Tsang-chü ku-shih chi*, Peking 1963, pp. 120—49.

192. Topley (1954), p. 59.

193. The *Miao-ying pao-chüan*, for instance, spirits its threatened heroine away in a storm of wind, like Miao-shan of the first-stage versions. Liu Hsiang and Mei-shih, in the *pao-chüan* of their names, also escape death.

194. Such a complex is common to *Huang-shih nü pao-chüan*, *Hsiu-nü pao-chüan*, *Yü-ying pao-chüan*.

195. This remains so even though the complex serves different specific purposes in different texts. The rebirth of Huang-shih usefully transfers her to the privileged male status which she has earned by religious merit

and which gives her the secular authority to put her family affairs to rights. But the resurrection of Hsiu-nü or Yü-ying serves no such rational or utilitarian purpose.

196. *Fo-shuo fu-mu en nan-pao ching*, 778—9. The translation of this text, listed as anonymous in early catalogues, was only from T'ang times attributed to An Shih-kao (*fl.* A.D. 147—70), and its provenance is thus open to suspicion. See Michihata Ryōshū, p. 70.

197. See E. Burnouf, *Introduction à l'histoire du buddhisme indien*, Paris 1844, p. 270. The passage quoted is translated from Burnouf's version of the *Purṇāvadāna* section of the collection.

198. *Yü-lan-p'en ching shu*, 505a. The background and broader implications of this material and the relationship between Buddhist and Confucian ethics in general are examined in Michihata Ryōshū (1968), especially on pp. 219—47. See also Kenneth K.S. Ch'en, *The Chinese transformation of Buddhism*, Princeton 1973, pp. 18 ff.

199. See above, ch. 3.5.

200. First edition, Paris 1909; currently available English version, trans. M.B. Vizedom and G.L. Caffee, *The rites of passage*, London 1960.

201. From the English version, p. 11. Cf. van Gennep's original phrasing: '*Rites de séparation, Rites de marge, et Rites d'agrégation*' (1909 edn., p. 14).

202. *Les rites de passage* (1909), ch. 6, pp. 93—163. Both before and since van Gennep's time there has been a vast ethnographic literature on the subject of initiation. A further sampling of earlier reports appears in the article 'Initiation' in James Hastings, ed., *Encyclopaedia of religion and ethics*, vol. 7, Edinburgh 1914, pp. 314—29. Later works are cited by Mircea Eliade in *Birth and rebirth: the religious meanings of initiation in human culture* (trans. W.R. Trask), London 1961, *passim*.

203. The doctrinal background of the rites, their nature and their current social context are described and illustrated in Welch (1967), pp. 179—205.

204. See de Groot (1885), *passim*; Doolittle, vol. 1, pp. 191 ff.; Topley (1952), and (1958), pp. 293 ff. For a rich fictional documentation of mourning ritual practice in North China, see *Chin P'ing Mei tz'u-hua*, 6.1b, 7.10a, 8.10ab, 16.9a, 59.17ab, 62.6a, 63.7b, 65.1ab, 4ab, 66, *passim*, 68.1b—2b, 78.21a, 80.1ab, 6a—8a.

205. Variously known as *shih-o-kuei, shih-shih, fang-yen-k'ou, p'u-tu ku-hun, shang-t'ai*.

206. For an assessment of Ti-tsang's role in the Chinese Hell, see Sawada Mizuho (1968), pp. 113 ff.

207. Katō, p. 413; *T*. 9.58a; Kern, p. 415.

208. The *sūtra* (*T*. 20, no. 1050) was translated into Chinese in the tenth century. For the episodes in Hell, see 48b—49b. The full contents are summarised by Marie-Thérèse de Mallmann in *Introduction à l'étude d'Avalokiteçvara*. Paris 1948, pp. 39—47. Relevant parts are translated from the Nepalese Sanskrit version by E.B. Cowell in 'The Northern Buddhist legend of Avalokiteswara's descent into the hell Avichi', *Journal of Philology* 6, 1876, 222—31. A comparable episode in Taoist mythology is told in the *T'ai-shang chiu-chen miao-chieh chin-lu tu-ming pa-tsui*

miao-ching; cf. Yoshioka Yoshitoyo (1959), pp. 378—82.

209. On the term *preta*, in which the literal meaning 'departed' is confused with another term *pitara* ('father' or ancestral spirit), see Richard F. Gombrich, *Precept and practice: traditional Buddhism in the rural highlands of Ceylon*, Oxford 1971, p. 163; also Welch (1967), pp. 179—83, dealing also with the concept of Orphaned Souls.

210. A detailed account of the textual history of 'Hungry Ghosts' ritual in China is given in Yoshioka (1959) pp. 369—432.

211. The most influential liturgical version is the revision of 1606 by Chu-hung (1535—1615): see *Hsiu-she yü-ch'ieh chi-yao shih-shih t'an-i* and other related texts gathered in the same volume of Z. For further data, see Yoshioka (1959), pp. 419—24, and Chun-jo Liu, 'The serendipity chants, a descriptive catalogue of the recordings of the Buddhist rite for the dead, "Yü-chia yen-k'ou shih-shih yao chi" ', *Chinoperl News* 3, 1973.

212. Various descriptions of the physical circumstances of the rite can be found in de Groot (1886), pp. 430—2; Doolittle, vol. 2, pp. 95 ff.; Welch (1967), pp. 185 ff.; K.L. Reichelt, *Truth and tradition in Chinese Buddhism*, rev. edn., Shanghai 1934, pp. 89 ff.; Topley (1952), pp. 157—8, and (1958), pp. 299 ff. (the latter with a diagram of the layout on the ceremonial table). I have myself witnessed performances of this rite, by various different teams of religious practitioners, among different dialect groups, both in public *Yü-lan* celebrations and in private mourning ceremonies, during the summer of 1973 in Hong Kong, Singapore and Penang.

213. See Welch (1967), p. 490, n. 10; W. Perceval Yetts, 'Notes on the disposal of Buddhist dead in China', *Journal of the Royal Asiatic Society*, 1911, pp. 701—3; illustration in de Groot (1903), plate III.

214. *Hsiu-she yü-ch'ieh chi-yao shih-shih t'an-i*, 404a; Chun-jo Liu, pp. 21, 57, 91.

215. *Hsiu-she yü-ch'ieh chi-yao shih-shih t'an-i*, 405a.

216. See the illustrations included in the texts *Yü-ch'ieh shih-shih chi-yao*, 457a, and *Yü-ch'ieh yen-k'ou chu-chi tsuan-yao*, 481b—482a.

217. Bronislaw Malinowski, 'Myth as a dramatic development of dogma', in *Sex, culture and myth*, London 1963, p. 251. For a fuller statement, see his *Myth in primitive psychology*, London 1926, in particular the following passage: 'Myth is not only looked upon as a commentary of additional information, but it is a warrant, a charter, and often even a practical guide to the activities with which it is connected. On the other hand the rituals, ceremonies, customs, and social organization contain at times direct references to myth, and they are regarded as the results of a mythical event. The cultural fact is a monument in which the myth is embodied; while the myth is believed to be the real cause which has brought about the moral rule, the social grouping, the rite, or the custom' (pp. 37—8).

218. For an account of the documentary background to the story of Mu-lien and his connection with the *Yü-lan* rituals, see Iwamoto Yutaka (1968); also Michihata Ryōshū, pp. 114—21; Sawada Mizuho (1968), pp. 128—48.

Appendix

Note

THIS appendix properly consists of a comparative table of proper names and other narrative features used in different versions of the story. For the reader's convenience it is printed on the end-paper at the close of the volume. No attempt is made to list out all names and narrative features appearing in the various versions: to do so would use up space to no purpose. The aim of this table is to supplement the argument in the text above by bringing together those features which can be meaningfully and usefully compared. Those which have no comparative value are omitted.

The following abbreviations are used in the table:

Tsu: version by Tsu-hsiu
Chüeh: version by Chüeh-lien
Kuan: version by Kuan Tao-sheng
Hsiang: *Hsiang-shan pao-chüan*, as reprinted in Yoshioka (1971)
Nan: *Nan-hai Kuan-yin ch'üan-chuan*
Tseng: *Ch'u-hsiang tseng-pu sou-shen chi ta-ch'üan*
San: *San-chiao yüan-liu sheng-ti fo-tsu sou-shen ta-ch'üan*
Fu: *Hsiang-shan chi* (Fu-ch'un t'ang edn.)
Pen: *Kuan-yin chi-tu pen-yüan chen-ching*

List of Works Cited

The works listed here, subdivided into Abbreviations, Primary and Secondary Sources, include the most frequently cited works in Western languages and the great majority of those in Chinese and Japanese. Bibliographical details of all works not included are provided in relevant footnotes throughout the book.

Abbreviations
Nan-hai   *Nan-hai Kuan-yin ch'üan-chuan:* see ch.4.1. and n.80.
San-chiao yüan-liu   *San-chiao yüan-liu sheng-ti fo-tsu sou-shen ta-ch'üan:* see ch.4.2. and n.106.
T.   *Taishō shinshū daizōkyō* 大正新脩大藏經.
Tseng-pu sou-shen chi   *Ch'u-hsiang tseng-pu sou-shen chi ta-ch'üan:* see ch.4.2. and n.105.
Z.   *Dai Nippon zokuzōkyō* 大日本續藏經.

Primary Sources
The sign § is placed before individual items in a given work which are cited in the text.
Ch'a-hsiang shih hsü-ch'ao 茶香室續鈔. By Yü Yüeh 俞樾 (1821–1907). In *Ch'un-tsai t'ang ch'üan-shu* 春在堂全書, rev. edn., 1899.
Ch'a-hsiang shih ts'ung-ch'ao 茶香室叢鈔. By Yü Yüeh. In *Ch'un-tsai t'ang ch'üan-shu*, 1899.
Chi-ku ko chen-ts'ang pi-pen shu-mu 汲古閣珍藏祕本書目. By Mao I 毛扆 (1640–1710+). In *Shih-li chü ts'ung-shu* 士禮居叢書.
Chi Shen-chou san-pao kan-t'ung lu 集神州三寶感通錄. By Tao-hsüan 道宣 (596–667). T. 52, no.2106.
Ch'ien-tao Lin-an chih 乾道臨安志. By Chou Ts'ung 周淙. In *Yüeh-ya t'ang ts'ung-shu* 粵雅堂叢書.

List of Works Cited

Chin P'ing Mei tz'u-hua 金瓶梅詞話. Facsimile of Wan-li edn., Daian, Tokyo 1963.

Ch'in-ting ssu-k'u ch'üan-shu tsung-mu 欽定四庫全書總目. (Submitted to the throne in 1782.) Facsimile reprint, Taipei 1964.

Ch'in-ting Ta-Ch'ing hui-tien 欽定大清會典. Edn. of 1764.

Ch'ü-hai tsung-mu t'i-yao 曲海總目提要. Peking 1959.

Ch'ü-lu 曲錄. By Wang Kuo-wei 王國維 (1877—1927). In *Hai-ning Wang Ching-an hsien-sheng i-shu* 海寧王靜安先生遺書.

Ch'ü Wei chiu-wen 曲洧舊聞. By Chu Pien 朱弁 (d. 1148). In *Hsüeh-chin t'ao-yüan* 學津討源.

Fo-shuo fu-mu en nan-pao ching 佛說父母恩難報經 T. 16, no.684.

Fo-tsu li-tai t'ung-tsai 佛祖歷代通載. By Nien-ch'ang 念常 (d. 1341). T. 49, no.2036.

Ho-nan t'ung-chih 河南通志. By T'ien Wen-ching 田文鏡 et al. Edn. of 1869.

Hsi-yu chi 西遊記. Repr. Tso-chia ch'u-pan she, Peking 1954.

Hsiao-shih chin-kang k'o-i hui-yao chu-chieh 銷釋金剛科儀會要註解. Ed. Chüeh-lien 覺連 (preface dated 1551). Z. 1, 1, 92, 2.

Hsin-pien Tsui-weng t'an-lu 新編醉翁談錄. By Chin Ying-chih 金盈之. Modern reprint, Shanghai 1958.

Hsiu-she yü-ch'ieh chi-yao shih-shih t'an-i 修設瑜伽集要施食壇儀. By Chu-hung 袾宏 (1535—1615). Z. 1,2,9,5,396b—415a.

Hsü tzu-chih t'ung-chien ch'ang-pien 續資治通鑑長編. By Li Tao 李燾 (1115—1184). Che-chiang shu-chü 浙江書局 edn., 1881.

Hua-p'in 畫品. By Li Chien 李薦 (1059—1109). In *Mei-shu ts'ung-shu* 美術叢書.

Ju-chou ch'üan-chih 汝州全志. By Po Ming-i 白明義 et al. Edn. of 1840.

§ 'Ch'ung-hsiu Hsiang-shan Kuan-yin ta-shih t'a chi' 重修香山觀音大士塔記, by Liu Jo-tsai 劉若宰 : 10.44b—46a.

Ku-pen hsi-ch'ü ts'ung-k'an 古本戲曲叢刊. Second Series, Shanghai 1955; Third Series, Peking 1957.

Kuan Yao-wang Yao-shang erh p'u-sa ching 觀藥王藥上二菩薩經. T. 20, no.1161.

Kuei-ssu lei-kao 癸巳類稿. By Yü Cheng-hsieh 俞正燮 (1775—1840). Repr. Shanghai 1957.

§ 'Kuan-shih-yin p'u-sa chuan-lüeh pa' 觀世音菩薩傳略跋: 15.570—6.

§ 'Kuan-shih-yin p'u-sa ming-i k'ao' 觀世音菩薩名義考 : 15.576—9.

Li pa-shih-pa fo hung-ming pao-ch'an 禮八十八佛洪名寶懺. Ed. Tao-p'ei 道霈 (preface dated 1664). Repr. Jui-ch'eng shu-chü, Taichung 1955.

Liu Hsiang pao-chüan 劉香寶卷. Blockprint edition of 1851.

Lung-hsing Fo-chiao pien-nien t'ung-lun 隆興佛教編年通論. By Tsu-hsiu 祖琇. Z. 1, 2B, 3, 3—4.

Lü-ch'uang nü-shih 綠窗女史. Late Ming edition.

Ming-shih 明史. Modern repr. Peking 1974.
Naikaku bunko Kanseki bunrui mokuroku 内閣文庫漢籍分類目錄. Tokyo 1956.
Pao-feng hsien-chih 寶豐縣志. By Wu I 武億 and Lu Jung 陸蓉. Edn. of 1797.
　§ 'Ch'ung-chien Ju-chou Hsiang-shan Kuan-yin ch'an-yüan chi' 重建汝州香山觀音禪院記: 16.4a—6b.
　§ 'Ju-chou Hsiang-shan Ta-pei p'u-sa chuan' 汝州香山大悲菩薩傳, by Chiang Chih-ch'i 蔣之奇: 15.7a—8a.
　§ 'Po-ch'üeh ssu k'ao' 白雀寺考, by Po Hung 白鉉: 10.2a—4a.
　§ 'Tu-hsiu ti-wu chi Ta-pei t'a chi' 獨修第五級大悲塔記: 15.6b—7a.
　§ 'Tz'u-shou yüan-chu Chung-hai shang-jen ling-t'a chih' 慈壽院主重海上人靈塔誌: 15.4b—5a.
Pao-feng hsien-chih 寶豐縣志. By Keng Hsing-tsung 耿興宗 and Li Fang-wu 李彷梧. Edn. of 1837.
　§ 'Ch'ung-hsiu Po-ch'üeh ssu chi' 重修白雀寺記, by Li Hung-chih 李宏志: 15.15b—17a.
Shao-shih shan-fang pi-ts'ung 少室山房筆叢. By Hu Ying-lin 胡應麟 (1551—1602). Shanghai 1958 edn.
Sui-shu 隋書. Modern repr., Peking 1973.
Sung-hsüeh chai wen-chi 松雪齋文集. By Chao Meng-fu 趙孟頫 (1254—1322). In *Ssu-pu ts'ung-k'an* 四部叢刊, First Series.
　§ 'Wei-kuo fu-jen Kuan-shih mu-chih ming' 魏國夫人管氏墓誌銘: *wai-chi* 外集, 18ab.
Sung-shih 宋史. *Ssu-pu ts'ung-k'an Po-na* edn.
Ta-Ming i-t'ung ming-sheng chih 大明一統名勝志. Edn. of 1630.
Ta-T'ang San-tsang ch'ü-ching shih-hua 大唐三藏取經詩話. Photographic facsimile edn. by Lo Chen-yü 羅振玉, 1916. Modern reprint, Peking 1955.
T'ai-shang chiu-chen miao-chieh chin-lu tu-ming pa-tsui miao-ching 太上九真妙戒金籙度命拔罪妙經. *Tao-tsang* 道藏, fasc.77.
Tao-hsüan Lü-shih kan-t'ung lu 道宣律師感通錄. By Tao-hsüan (596—667). T. 52, no.2107.
Ts'ung-jung lu 從容錄. By Cheng-chüeh 正覺 (1091—1157) and Hsing-hsiu 行秀 (1156—1236, or 1166—1246). T. 48, no.2004.
T'ung-chih 通志. By Cheng Ch'iao 鄭樵 (1104—1162). Commercial Press edn., Shanghai 1935.
Yü-ch'ieh shih-shih chi-yao 瑜伽施食集要. Z. 1, 2, 9, 5, 447b—467b.
Yü-ch'ieh yen-k'ou chu-chi tsuan-yao 瑜伽燄口註集纂要. Z. 1, 2, 9, 5, 468a—492b.
Yü-lan-p'en ching shu 盂蘭盆經疏. By Tsung-mi 宗密 (780—841). T. 39, no. 1792.
Yüan-shan t'ang ch'ü-p'in 遠山堂曲品. By Ch'i Piao-chia 祁彪佳 (1602—1645). In *Chung-kuo ku-tien hsi-ch'ü lun-chu chi-ch'eng* 中國古典戲曲論著集成, vol. 6, Peking 1959.

Secondary Sources

A-YING 阿英 (pseud. of Ch'ien Hsing-ts'un 錢杏邨). *Chung-kuo lien-huan t'u-hua shih-hua* 中國連環圖畫史話. Peking 1957.
BOXER, C.R. (ed.) *South China in the sixteenth century, being the narratives of Galeote Pereira, Fr. Gaspar da Cruz, O.P., Fr. Martín de Rada, O.E.S.A. (1550—1575)*. Hakluyt Society, London 1953.
CHAPIN, Helen B. 'A long roll of Buddhist images — IV' (revised by Alexander C. Soper), *Artibus Asiae* 33, 1971, 75—142. Repr. in book form: *A long roll of Buddhist images*, Ascona 1972, pp.135—202.
CHENG Chen-to 鄭振鐸. 'Fo-ch'ü hsü-lu' 佛曲叙錄. Reprinted in *Chung-kuo wen-hsüeh yen-chiu* 中國文學研究, Peking 1957, pp.1068—1101.
CHENG Chen-to. *Hsi-ti shu-mu* 西諦書目. Peking 1963.
CHENG Ch'ien 鄭騫. 'Ming Ssu Kan-hsüan pen *P'i-p'a chi*' 明斯干軒本琵琶記. Reprinted in his *Ching-wu ts'ung-pien* 景午叢編, Taipei 1972, vol. 2, pp. 439—44.
CH'IEN Nan-yang 錢南揚 (ed.) *P'i-p'a chi* 琵琶記, editor's preface. Peking 1960.
CHOU Tso-jen 周作人. 'Liu Hsiang nü' 劉香女. Reprinted in his *Kua-tou chi* 瓜豆集, Shanghai 1937, pp. 42—51.
CHOU Yüeh-jan 周越然. *Shu shu shu* 書書書. Shanghai 1944, reprinted Hong Kong 1966.
DE GROOT, J.J.M. 'Buddhist masses for the dead in Amoy'. *Actes du Sixième Congrés International des Orientalistes*, Pt. 4, sect. 4, Leiden 1885, 1—120.
DE GROOT J.J.M. *Les fêtes annuellement célébrées à Emoui* (trans. C.G. Chavannes). Annales du Musée Guimet, Bibliothèque d'études, 11—12, Paris 1886.
DE GROOT, J.J.M. *Sectarianism and religious persecution in China*, Amsterdam 1903—4.
DOOLITTLE, Justus. *Social life of the Chinese*. New York 1865.
DORÉ, Henri. *Recherches sur les superstitions en Chine*, IIme partie: *Le panthéon chinois*, vol. 6. Variétés Sinologiques 39, Shanghai 1914.
DUDBRIDGE, Glen. 'The hundred-chapter *Hsi-yu chi* and its early versions'. *Asia Major*, New Series, 14, 1969, 141—91.
Fu Hsi-hua 傅惜華. 'Pao-chüan tsung-lu' 寶卷總錄. *Han-hsüeh lun-ts'ung* 漢學論叢 (*Mélanges Sinologiques*), Peking 1951, 41—103.
GETTY, Alice. *The gods of Northern Buddhism*. Second edition. Oxford 1928.
IWAMOTO Yutaka 岩本裕. *Mokuren densetsu to Urabon* 目連傳說と盂蘭盆. Kyoto 1968.
KATŌ Bunnō (trans.). *Myōhō-renge-kyō: The Sutra of the Lotus Flower of the Wonderful Law*. Revised by W.E. Soothill and Wilhelm Schiffer. Tokyo 1971.
KERN, Jan Hendrik (trans.). *The Saddharma-pundarîka, or the Lotus of the True Law*. Sacred Books of the East, vol. 21. Oxford 1909.

KOBAYASHI Taichirō 小林太市郎. 'Tōdai no Daihi Kannon' 唐代の大悲觀音. Bukkyō geijutsu 佛教藝術 20, 1953, 3—27; 21, 1954, 89—109; 22, 1954, 3—28.

LAMOTTE, Etienne,'Mañjuśrī', T'oung Pao, S. 2, 48, 1960, 1—96.

LI Hsien-chang 李獻璋. 'Sankyō sōjin daizen to Tempi jōboden o chūshin to suru Boso densetsu no kōsatsu' 三教搜神大全と天妃娘媽傳を中心とする媽祖傳説の考察. Tōyō gakuhō 東洋學報 39, 1956, 76—108.

LI Shih-yü 李世瑜. 'Pao-chüan hsin-yen' 寶卷新研 Wen-hsüeh i-ch'an tseng-k'an 文學遺産增刊 4, Peking 1957, 165—81.

LI Shih-yü. Pao-chüan tsung-lu 寶卷綜録. Peking 1961.

LI T'ien-i 李田意. 'Jih-pen so-chien Chung-kuo tuan-p'ien hsiao-shuo lüeh-chi' 日本所見中國短篇小説略記. Ch'ing-hua hsüeh-pao 清華學報, New Series, 1. 2, 1957, 63—81.

LIU Hsiu-yeh 劉修業. Ku-tien hsiao-shuo hsi-ch'ü ts'ung-k'ao 古典小説戲曲叢考. Peking 1958.

LIU Ts'un-yan. Chinese popular fiction in two London libraries. Hong Kong 1967.

LU Hsün 魯迅 (pseud. of Chou Shu-jen 周樹人). 'Hou-chi' 後記. In Chao-hua hsi-shih 朝花夕拾. Reprinted in Lu Hsün ch'üan-chi 魯迅全集, Peking 1973, vol 2.

MA Yau-woon 馬幼垣. 'Hsiung Lung-feng so-k'an tuan-p'ien hsiao-shuo ssu-chung k'ao-shih' 熊龍峯所刊短篇小説四種考釋. Ch'ing-hua hsüeh-pao 清華學報, New Series, 7. 1, 1968, 257—78.

MICHIHATA Ryōshū 道端良秀. Bukkyō to Jukyō rinri 仏教と儒教理論. Kyoto 1968.

MOCHIZUKI Shinkō 望月信亨. Bukkyō daijiten 佛教大辭典. Tokyo 1936—7.

NAGASAWA Kikuya 長澤規矩也. 'Mindai gikyoku kankōsha-hyō shokō' 明代戲曲刊行者表初稿. Shoshigaku 書誌學 7, 1936, 2—9.

ŌTA Tatsuo 太田辰夫. 'Dai Tō Sanzō shukyō shiwa kō' 大唐三藏取經詩話考. Kōbe gaidai ronsō 神戸外大論叢 17, 1966, 135—60.

PEI-ying 北嬰 (pseud.). Ch'ü-hai tsung-mu t'i-yao pu-pien 曲海總目提要補編. Peking 1959.

SAEKI Tomi 佐伯富. 'Kinsei Chūgoku ni okeru Kannon shinkō 近世中國における觀音信仰. In Tsukamoto hakushi shōju kinen Bukkyōshigaku ronshū 塚本博士頌壽記念佛教史學論集, Kyoto 1961, pp. 372—89.

SAKAI Tadao 酒井忠夫. Chūgoku zensho no kenkyū 中國善書の研究. Tokyo 1960.

SAWADA Mizuho 澤田瑞穗. 'Raso no Muikyō' 羅祖の無為教, Part 1. Tōhō shūkyō 東方宗教 1, 1951, 44—63.

SAWADA Mizuho. 'Kimpeibai shiwa shoin no hōken ni tsuite' 金瓶梅詞話所引の寶卷について. Chūgoku bungaku hō 中國文學報 5, 1956, 86—98.

SAWADA Mizuho. Hōken no kenkyū 寶卷の研究. Nagoya 1963.

List of Works Cited

SAWADA Mizuho. 'Daruma-den shōsetsu' 達摩伝小説. Biblia 27, 1964, 9—12.
SAWADA Mizuho. 'Shakkyōgeki joroku' 釋教劇叙錄. Tenri daigaku gakuhō 天理大學學報 44, 1964, 21—43.
SAWADA Mizuho. 'Hōken to Bukkyō setsuwa' 寳卷と佛教説話. Bukkyō shigaku 佛教史學 11. 3—4, 1964, 177—94.
SAWADA Mizuho. En-Chō yawa: Saihō Kahoku densetsu shū 燕趙夜話―採訪華北傳説集 Nagoya 1965.
SAWADA Mizuho. Jigokuhen: Chūgoku no meikaisetsu 地獄變―中國の冥界説. Kyoto 1968.
SUN K'ai-ti 孫楷第. Chung-kuo t'ung-su hsiao-shuo shu-mu 中國通俗小説書目. Second edition. Peking 1957.
SUN K'ai-ti. Jih-pen Tung-ching so-chien hsiao-shuo shu-mu 日本東京所見小説書目. Second edition. Peking 1958.
SUZUKI Chūsei 鈴木中正. 'Sōdai Bukkyō kessha no kenkyū' 宋代佛教結社の研究. Shigaku zasshi 史學雜誌 52, 1941, 65—98, 205—41, 303—33.
SUZUKI Chūsei. 'Rakyō ni tsuite' 羅教について. Tōyō bunka kenkyūjo kiyō 東洋文化研究所紀要 1, 1943, 441—501.
TOPLEY, Marjorie. 'Chinese rites for the repose of the soul, with special reference to Cantonese custom'. Journal of the Malayan Branch of the Royal Asiatic Society 25, 1952, 149—60.
TOPLEY, Marjorie. 'Chinese women's vegetarian houses in Singapore'. Journal of the Malayan Branch of the Royal Asiatic Society 27, 1954, 51—67.
TOPLEY, Marjorie. 'The organization and social function of Chinese women's Chai-t'ang in Singapore'. Unpublished Ph.D. dissertation, University of London, 1958.
TOPLEY, Marjorie. 'The Great Way of Former Heaven: A group of Chinese secret religious sects'. Bulletin of the School of Oriental and African Studies 26, 1963, 362—92.
TSUKAMOTO Zenryū 塚本善隆. 'Kinsei Shina taishū no joshin Kannon shinkō' 近世シナ大衆の女身觀音信仰. In Yamaguchi hakushi kanreki kinen Indogaku Bukkyōgaku ronshū 山口博士還曆記念印度學佛教學論集, Kyoto 1955, 262—80.
WALEY, Arthur D. 'Avalokiteśvara and the legend of Miao-shan'. Artibus Asiae 1, 1925, 130—2.
WALEY, Arthur D. Catalogue of paintings recovered from Tun-huang by Sir Aurel Stein. London 1931.
WANG Ch'ing-cheng 汪慶正. 'Chi wen-hsüeh, hsi-ch'ü ho pan-hua shih shang ti i-tz'u chung-yao fa-hsien' 記文學戲曲和版畫史上的一次重要發現. Wen-wu 文物 1973, 11, 58—67.
WELCH, Holmes. The practice of Chinese Buddhism, 1900—1950. Harvard East Asian Studies 26. Cambridge, Massachusetts, 1967.
YOSHIOKA Yoshitoyo 吉岡義豊. Dōkyō no kenkyū 道教の研究. Kyoto 1952.
YOSHIOKA Yoshitoyo. Dōkyō to Bukkyō 道教と佛教. Vol. 1.

Tokyo 1959.

YOSHIOKA Yoshitoyo. 'Shōshaku kongō kagi no seiritsu ni tsuite' 銷釋金剛科儀の成立について. *Ryūkoku shidan* 龍谷史壇 56—57, 1966, 154—70.

YOSHIOKA Yoshitoyo. 'Kenryūban *Kōzan hōken* kaisetsu' 乾隆版香山寶卷解說. *Dōkyō kenkyū* 道教研究 4, 1971, 115—95.

Index

Act of Truth, 76
Amitābha, 67
An Shih-kao 安世高
  (fl. 147—70), n.196
Aśoka, 78
Avalokiteśvara (see also Kuan-yin),
  8, 78; n.21
Avīci hell, 94, 97

Bodhidharma, ārya, 達摩尊者,
  70—1

Canton, 67
celibacy, 25, 40, 85 ff.
Chang Ta-fu 張大復, 68—9
Chao Meng-fu 趙孟頫, 39
Chao Pi 趙佖 (d. 1106), n.63
Ch'ao-yüan tung 朝元洞,
  (P'u-t'o shan), 69
che-ku-t'ien 鷓鴣天, tune, 55;
  n.86
Ch'en Kuang-jui 陳光蕊, 56;
  n.92
Cheng-chüeh 正覺
  (1091—1157), 36
Ch'eng-hsin hsien 澄心縣, 49
Ch'i Piao-chia 祁彪佳
  (1602—45), 62, 65
Chiang Chih-ch'i 蔣之奇
  (1031—1104), 10, 12, 14—19,
  22, 24, 36, 43, 46—7, 74, 81—2
Chien-ning 建寧 (Fukien), 66
Chien-yang 建陽 (Fukien),
  52—3, 56, 60, 66

Chih-kung 智公, Buddhist monk,
  45
Chin-kang k'o-i, 25, 85; n.39
Chin P'ing Mei tz'u-hua, 46—7, 87;
  n.204
Chin Ying-chih 金盈之, 37
Ch'ing-liang shan 清涼山, 56;
  n.95
Chu-hung 袾宏 (1535—1615),
  n.211
Chu Pien 朱弁 (d. 1148), 14, 15,
  19, 20, 22 ff., 74
Chu Ting-ch'en, 52, 54—8, 60
Ch'u-hsiang tseng-pu Sou-shen chi
  ta-ch'üan, 58—62
ch'uan-ch'i 傳奇, dramatic
  genre, 53, 63
Chüeh-lien 覺連, 25 ff., 35—6,
  43, 49, 75, 82, 89
Chung-hai 重海 (d. 1051), 11
Chung-nan shan 終南山
  (Shensi), 12, 13, 17, 22, 25;
  n.23
Citadel of the Unjustly Dead
  (Wang-ssu ch'eng 枉死城)
  (see also under Hungry Ghosts),
  64
Cruz, Gaspar da, (d. 1570), 67

Divyāvadāna, Buddhist Sanskrit
  text, 90

elephant, 55—6
execution, 40, 43, 48, 50, 63, 82, 88

Fan Ch'iung 范瓊, 12
fang-yen-k'ou 放 燄 口
 (cf. Hungry Ghosts, Feeding of),
 95; n.205
Feng-tu 酆都, Underworld, 41
fifty-three salutations, 64; n.131
filial piety, 89—91, 94—7,
fish, grateful, (motif in fiction), 56;
 n.92
five-pointed crown (used in Hungry
 Ghosts ritual), 95
Forest of Corpses (Shih-to-lin 屍多
 林), 48, 59, 83
Fu-ch'eng hsien 父城縣
 (Honan), n.41
Fu-ch'un t'ang 富春堂, Nanking
 publishing firm, 59, 62, 65
Fukien, 7, 52, 60, 66

Gadgadasvara (see also Miao-yin),
 78
Golden Boy and Jade Girl 金童玉
 女, 64
gṛhapati ('householder', Skt.), 54,
 60

Hai-ch'ao yin, 68
Hai-yin 海印, n.63
Hangchow, 45, 47
Hell, 43, 48, 61, 63, 66, 72, 83—4,
 88—9, 92—7
Hou hsing-che 猴行者, 38
Hsi-chien 喜見 (see also under
 Yao-wang), 76
Hsi-yang chi (attrib. Lo Mao-teng),
 n.105
Hsi-yu chi, 38, 54—8, 60
Hsiang-shan 香山, n.12 et
 passim; — chi, 62—5, 82—3, 92;
 — chüan, 44—5; — pao-chüan,
 45 ff., 56—60, 66, 68, 81, 85; —
 ssu 寺, 11, 13—4, 16—20,
 24—5, 36, 38, 42; n.32
hsien-jen 仙人 (Skt. ṛṣi), 75
Hsien-t'ien ta-tao 先天大道,
 69—72
Hsing-hsiu 行秀 (1156—1236),
 36—7
Hsing-lin 興林, kingdom of King
 Miao-chuang, 49

Hsiung Lung-feng 熊龍峯,
 publisher, 60; n.116
hsü-pan 序班, palace
 functionary, 46
Hsüan-tsang 玄奘 (d. 664), 38
Hu Ying-lin 胡應麟
 (1551—1602), 19
Huai-chou 懷晝, abbot of
 Hsiang-shan ssu, 12, 14—17, 81
Huang-shih nü chüan, 87—8
Hui-chen 惠真, 29
Hui-chou 惠州 (Kwangtung), 49
Hung-hai-erh 紅孩兒, demon,
 n.101
Hungry Ghosts, 94—5; Feeding of
 —, 94 ff.; Citadel of —, 94
Huo-chu shan 火珠山
 (cf. Lung-shan), 10

I-ch'ang 義常, disciple of
 Tao-hsüan, 13—14, 16
initiation, 93

Jade Girl, see under Golden Boy
Jātaka literature, 75, 90
Ju-chou 汝州 (Honan), 10—12,
 14, 16, 18, 23—4, 47, 49

Kāmalā ('jaundice', Skt.), 23, 31,
 35, 49, 75
Kāraṇḍavyūhasūtra, 94; n.208
karma, 82—3
King Lear, 79
Kṣitigarbha, see under Ti-tsang
ku-hun 孤魂, see under
 Orphaned Souls
Kuan Tao-sheng 管道昇
 (1262—1319), 39—40, 46, 48—9,
 82
Kuan-tzu-tsai 觀自在
 (cf. Kuan-yin), 95
Kuan-yin 觀音, cult of, 15,
 18—9, 24—5, 67—8; female —,
 8—9, 15; iconography of —,
 10 ff., 56; n.90, 94; — in 'Hungry
 Ghosts' ritual, 94—6; Ta-pei,
 10 ff., 36—7, 75—6; n.21
Kuang-yeh shan-jen 廣野山人,
 69—71
Kuei-men-kuan 鬼門關, 64

Index

Kuan-yin chi-tu pen-yüan chen-ching, 69—73

Li Chien 李薦 (1059—1109), 12, 16
Ling-kan ssu 靈感寺, 13, 25
lion, of Mañjuśrī, 55—6; n.93
Liu Hsiang pao-chüan, 86; n.190
Lo-chiao 羅教, sectarian religious complex, n.59
Lo Ch'ing 羅清 (1443?—1527), n.59
Lo Mao-teng 羅懋登, 59, 62
Loarca, Miguel de, 7, 66—8; n.2
Lotus sūtra, 64—5, 76—79, 90, 94
Lu-shan 廬山, 45
luan-t'an 亂彈, local theatrical genre, n.134
Lung-men 龍門 (Honan), n.47
Lung-nü 龍女, dragon king's daughter, 55—6
Lung-shan 龍山 (Honan), 10—11
Lü 律, Buddhist sect, 14—16; — Master, see under Tao-hsüan

Ma-tsu 媽祖, goddess, 60
Malinowski, Bronislaw, 96
Mañjuśrī, bodhisattva, 17, 38, 56; n.25, 95
Mao Chin 毛晉 (1599—1659), 59
marriage, 7, 25, 27, 40, 79—81, 85 ff.
Maudgalyāyana, see under Mu-lien
Medicine-King, see under Yao-wang
Mendoza, Juan González de, 8
Miao-chuang, King, 49, 54; reign-title, 49
Miao-chuang-yen 妙莊嚴 (Skt. Śubhavyūha), king and father of Miao-shan, 14, 18, 22, 26, 35, 40, 77, 79
Miao-shan, canonical references to, 78
Miao-yen, 23, 26, 78—9
Miao-yin (Skt. Gadgadasvara), 23, 26, 40, 78, 79
Miao-yüan 妙緣, 40
ming-tsan, palace functionary, 46; n.70

Mother, sectarian goddess, 70—1
Mu-lien 目連 (Skt. Maudgalyāyana), 90—1, 96—7; n.218

Nan-hai Kuan-yin ch'üan-chuan, 51—8, 59—60, 66, 70
Nan-shan, see under Chung-nan shan
nei-tan 內丹, branch of Taoist alchemy, 72—3

O-mei shan 峨眉山, Szechwan, n.95
Orphaned Souls (ku-hun), 94—6

pagoda, 10—11, 13, 15, 18, 23; n.9
pao-chüan 寶卷, 44—50, 69—70, 72, 87, 89
Pao-feng 寶峰, Buddhist monk, 45, 47
Pao-feng 寶豐 (Honan), 10-11, 35, 81
Pao-ying 寶應, mother of Miao-shan, 26
peaches, 41, 48, 83
Po-ch'üeh ssu 白雀寺, 11, 19, 29, 36, 40, 42, 48—9, 72—4; n.32
P'o Ch'ieh 婆伽, personal name of King Miao-chuang, 49
preta, 94; n.209
P'u-men p'in 普門品, chapter of Lotus sūtra, 64, 77
P'u-ming 普明, Buddhist monk, 45, 47
P'u-ting hsien-shih 普定仙師, 69
P'u-t'o shan 普陀山 (Chekiang), 56, 69
p'u-tu ku-hun 普度孤魂, cf. Feeding of Hungry Ghosts, n.205

Rada, Martín de, (1533—78), 7, 65—7
relics, 18, 23—5, 34, 42, 76—7; n.28
rites de passage, 92 ff.
ṛṣi, see under 'hsien-jen'

Sāgara, dragon king, n.90

Śākyamuni, Buddha, 60, 91
Samantabhadra, bodhisattva, 56; n.95
San-chiao yüan-liu sou-shen ta-ch'üan, 58—61
sects, 44, 50, 87
Shan-ssu lo-han 善思羅漢, 69
Shan-ts'ai 善財 (Skt. Sudhana), attendant of Kuan-yin, 55—6; n.90
shang-t'ai 上台, cf. Feeding of Hungry Ghosts, n.205
shih-o-kuei 施餓鬼, Feeding of Hungry Ghosts, n.205
Shih Shan 施善, preincarnation of Miao-shan, 60
shih-shih 施食, cf. Feeding of Hungry Ghosts, n.205
Shih-to-lin, see under Forest of Corpses
stūpa (cf. pagoda), 18, 23—5, 34, 42, 49, 74, 76—7; n.9
Śubhavyūha, see under Miao-chuang-yen
Sudhana, see under Shan-ts'ai
Sukhāvatī, Paradise, 94
Sumeru, Mount, 49
Sung, Mount, 嵩山, 18, 23, 26, 34
Śūraṅgamasūtra, 14; n.21

Ta-pei 大悲, *see under* Kuan-yin *and* pagoda
Ta-pei Kuan-yin ching 大悲觀音經, 14
Ta-shih 大士 (Skt. *Mahāsattva*), n.28; — kung 公, manifestation of Kuan-yin, 67
Ta T'ien-hsi 答天錫, n.30
T'ai-shan wang 泰山王, king of seventh court of Hell, n.161
Tao-hsüan 道宣 (596—667), 13, 16—7, 19, 22, 24—5, 35—6, 74, 82; n.23
Thousand arms and eyes, of Avalokiteśvara, 14, 16, 23—4, 33—4, 35, 38, 42, 49, 74, 76, 79
Ti-tsang 地藏 (Skt. Kṣitigarbha), 94
Tibet, 88

T'ien-chu ssu, Upper, 上天竺寺, 45
tiger, 40—1, 43, 63, 83
Tripitaka (San-tsang 三藏), 38, 56
Ts'ai Ching 蔡京 (d. 1126), 14, 16
Tsu-hsiu 祖琇, 22, 24—5, 35—6, 42—3, 49, 75, 82, 91
T'u-ti 土地, spirit, 63
Tz'u-shou yüan 慈壽院 (cf. Po-ch'üeh ssu), 11

Vairocana, Buddha, 95
Vaiśravaṇa, 38
van Gennep, Arnold, 92 ff.
vegetarianism, 27, 86—7, 89
Vimaladattā, n.167

Wang Shao 王劭 n.172
Wang-ssu ch'eng, *see under* Citadel of the Unjustly Dead
Wei-wei pu-tung T'ai-shan shen-ken chieh-kuo pao-chüan, 44
Wen-hsien 文獻, Sui empress, n.172
Wen-kung 文公, Buddhist monk, 45
Western Peak 西嶽, temple of, 60
women, social and ritual problems of, 71—2, 85 ff.
Wu Residence 吳府, n.63
Wu-t'ai shan 五臺山 (Shansi), 17; n.25, 95

Yama, king of Hell, 41, 63—4, 72, 88
Yang 楊, publishing family of Chien-yang, 52
Yao-ch'ih chin-mu 瑤池金母 (*see also* Mother), n.149
Yao-wang 藥王 ('Medicine-King'), Bodhisattva, 76—7
Yü-lan 盂蘭, rituals of seventh lunar month, 67, 95, 97; n.134
Yü-li chih-pao pien, n.161
Yün-men chuan 雲門傳, 58

CANISIUS COLLEGE LIBRARY
BQ4710.A84 C52
The legend of Miao-s

3 5084 00156 3793

BQ
4710
.A84
C52

DEC 2 '96

FEB 1 2 1992

CANISIUS COLLEGE LIBRARY
BUFFALO, N. Y.

DEMCO

	Tsu	Chüeh	Kuan	Hsiang
Pre-incarnate Miao-shan				
Father of same				
Country			西土	興林
King's name	莊嚴	妙莊嚴王	妙莊	婆伽
Reign title				妙莊
Queen	寶應	寶德		寶德
Daughter 1	妙顏	妙顏	妙因(音)	妙書
Daughter 2	妙音	妙音	妙緣	妙音
Daughter 3	妙善	妙善	妙善	妙善
Minister 1				張拱長
Minister 2				許智
Minister 3				劉欽
Minister 4				
Minister 5				
Location of Po-ch'üeh szu				汝州龍樹
Location of Hsiang-shan	嵩嶽之南二百里 SW of territory	嵩嶽之南二百餘里 SW of territory		惠州澄心
Son-in-law 1				
Son-in-law 2				
Abbess		惠真		
Soldiers				朱葉二侍
Instrument of death				弓絃
Rescuer	神	龍神	虎	虎
Forest				屍多林
Tempter Giver of peach				太白金星 帝
Description of Miao-shan on Hsiang-shan	菩薩	仙人	仙長	仙人
Monk-doctor				普怛囉
Master of same				悉怛多